W9-CDA-538

Aroma Heal 2

Aroma Heal 2

Powerful Techniques to Accelerate Inner Healing with Essential Oils

Christi Turley Diamond B.S., M.Ed.
Karisa Tomkinson B.S., M.S.

Disclaimer and Note to Readers

The material in this book is for informational purposes only. As each individual situation is unique, you should use proper discretion, in consultation with a healthcare practitioner, before undertaking the exercises and techniques described in this book. If you have any health problems, consult a Doctor before using this book. The authors and publisher expressly disclaim responsibility for any adverse effects that may result from the use or application of the book. It is not intended to prescribe, or treat any emotional or physical condition, illness or injury. Application of oils is solely at the discretion of the reader and any direction given in the book is merely a guideline for it's use. The authors, publishers or distributors of this book shall have no liability or responsibility to person or entity with respect to any and all alleged damage, loss or injury caused or alleged to be caused directly or indirectly by the information contained in this book. This book contains suggested use of oils based on acceptable dosage amounts. The author makes no claim to have verified or validated these suggestions. The readers must validate acceptable dosage amounts from the manufacturer before application. The information in this book is in no way intended as a substitute for medical advice and the authors recommend that all readers obtain medical advice from a licensed healthcare professional before using essential oils for any reason.

This document is geared towards providing exact and reliable information in regards to the topic and issue covered. The publication is sold with the idea that the publisher is not required to render accounting, officially permitted, or otherwise, qualified services. If advice is necessary, legal or professional, a practiced individual in the profession should be ordered.

-From a Declaration of Principles which was accepted and approved equally by a Committee of the American Bar Association and a Committee of Publishers and Associations.

In no way is it legal to reproduce, duplicate, or transmit any part of this document in either electronic means or in printed format. Recording of this publication is strictly prohibited and any storage of the document is not allowed unless with written permission from the publisher. All rights reserved.

The information provided herein is stated to be truthful and consistent, in that any liability, in terms of inattention or otherwise, by any usage or abuse of any policies, processes, or directions contained within is the solitary and utter responsibility of the recipient reader. Under no circumstances will any legal responsibility or blame be held against the publisher for any legal reparation, damages, or monetary loss due to the information herein, either directly or indirectly.

Respective authors own all copyrights not held by the publisher.

The information herein is offered for informational purposes solely, and is universal as so. The presentation of the information is without contract or any type of guarantee assurance.

The trademarks that are used are without any consent, and the publication of the trademark is without permission or backing by the trademark owner. All trademarks and brands within this book are for clarifying purposes only and are owned by the owners themselves, not affiliated with this document.

Dedication

I wouldn't be the woman I am today without the "feeling experiences" I have collected on my journey here in Earth School. As I've traveled this journey many people have walked into my life and left an imprint on my heart that shaped me into who I am today and I thank you for helping me experience love in its truest form and at its deepest level. I love you. I dedicate this book to God, for every day He brings me tender mercies that show me how ever aware He is of me, my life, and my needs; and because of Him I have my children who have taught me so much about myself and who have been my saving graces; I want to be more like them every day! I dedicate this book to Katie who is my ray of sunshine and teaches me how to love with all my heart and to live in the moment, to Caleb who teaches me to be comfortable in my own skin and fully accepting of self and others without judgment and to always have laughter and to bring joy to every moment possible, to Logan who is one of the hardest workers I know who teaches me that ANYTHING is possible when I set my mind to it and that great character makes you a natural leader, to Tyler who teaches me that our greatest gifts come from within ourselves and what God created us to be as we live our truth and to listen to our own inner knowing and that self love is the fastest way to create a place of peace within ourselves. I dedicate this book

to my husband and best friend Rick who has walked
the path of healing with me as we have cracked our
hearts wide open to each other and created the space
to live our dreams in a whole new realm and in a
world of love I've never experienced before. Rick,
your love and devotion keep me going and the
laughter and fun you bring to my life, has forever
transformed it for the better and I love that we are in
this together forever! You are the wind beneath my
wings. And of course my amazing friends who show
up at the perfect times to add sparkle to my life with
your love and nudges to help me remember who I am.
Your light strengthens mine. Thank you for shining
so brightly! I feel so blessed by the friends who have
walked into my life! I love you all!
-Christi

When life brings strong waves that could toss and
throw one around, it also brings great light, stability,
and guidance to assist in navigating through the
storm. Often for me, these lights in the storm have
been various angels who have come to my rescue,
provided direction, or comforted me in ways they or I
may not even be aware of. I dedicate this book to you.
These storms we experience cause an increase in
knowledge, wisdom, and understanding. They
provide greater insight to the thoughts, directions, and
choices we choose to act upon, implement, and
follow. Amidst all that we are taught in this life, my

constants never change. In all I do, I work, love, share, and serve because of my family. You have been my angels, my rocks, and my loves through everything. My two little angels are my strength and my love. Clara, you are my motivation and strength. You keep me moving, passionate, and enlivened with your excitement, energy, and fire for life and learning. You have a sparkle that is contagious. Gavin, you are my little love and logic. You help hold my hand and heart when it is tired and weak and lift me to move forward. Your little touch is healing beyond words. You ground me. You both help me to slow down and enjoy the little things. Tyler, my life is forever changed because of you. You have taught me so much about loving, serving, and standing strong. I have learned so much about myself throughout the years and I'm grateful for the teacher you are to me. I want to express my gratitude for the role you each have been in my life. I dedicate this book to you though, Clara, Gavin,...my angels.

-Karisa

Table of Contents:

Preface

We hope that you have familiarized yourself with our first book *Aroma Heal 1*. It provides a basic background of what energy healing is and how frequency and vibration can affect us. We explained a little about the limbic system (the emotional part of the brain) and how the oils work aromatically to create an environment of healing. We showed you how the two worlds of energy healing and essential oils marry each other perfectly to create the optimal environment for accelerating your own healing. We also shared four beautiful tools that can be used to initiate and create amazing healing in your life with relationships, stress, life experiences, and in many other ways.

In this book we will go a little deeper and delve a little further into energy healing. We provide you with more amazing tools to help you in healing the inner self and reinforce how to implement the use of essential oils to continue to accelerate that healing. We provide you with a substantial amount of fascinating scientific background on how it all works and the WHY behind it. In this book, we introduce you to five additional tools to powerfully enhance your toolbox for healing. Our focus in this book is YOU! To enable you to explore your own inner healing that will lead you to achieve the life and dreams you deserve! We will again specify which oils may be helpful for each exercise and walk you through each process step by step.

If you have any questions about how to get access to the essential oils we discuss within this book please contact either of us for more information:

Christi Diamond - Christi@thehealingcoach.com
Karisa Tomkinson - KarisaTomkinson@gmail.com

We look forward to sharing this journey with you!

Aroma Heal 2

Powerful Techniques to Accelerate Inner Healing with Essential Oils

Introduction

"If you feel lost, disappointed, hesitant, or weak,
return to yourself, to who you are, here and now, and
when you get there, you will discover yourself, like a
lotus flower in full bloom, even in a muddy pond,
beautiful and strong."
Masaru Emoto

What does it take to return to yourself? Who are
you really at your very core? When I work with my
clients, I describe to them my belief that when we are
born, we are a beautiful, bright light and perfect in
our own way. We are clean and free of any false
beliefs. We are pure and unspotted; a clean slate with
a full belief of our preciousness and free of anything
but the perfection we already are. I feel strongly that
we are born with a belief of knowing who we are. As
time goes by, this beautiful light starts to have
experiences in life and one by one a rock is placed
over the light. At first it's just one rock added, then,
another and another to a point where the light shining
through isn't very strong anymore. It is covered up or
weighed down by all the heavy rocks that become the
false beliefs we filter our lives through. I express to
my clients that those heavy rocks are just our belief
system (our B.S.) that we have taken on. So, in our
healing sessions, we are literally removing the false

beliefs that have often weighed us down for years. As we remove these rocks one by one, before long, that bright beautiful light that was always there starts shining through once again. The rocks no longer block its beauty or the strong beautiful light that came here to grow and shine stronger and brighter!

We believe so strongly in what we are sharing in this book because we use these tools successfully in our own lives. I personally participate in energy/essential oil healing sessions on a regular basis and the shifts I feel in my energy and in my life are amazing! It is liberating to let go of another block or belief that has held me prisoner for so long. I look forward to sharing my experiences with you in this book and the powerful growth that has come about for me and the clients I work with. Our hope is that in this book, you find the tools for your own inner healing and see transformation in your life so that you can discover your true self and the beautiful person you are and that from there we all create our own ripple effect on the world for greater good as our lights shine brighter and more brilliant!

Christi's Story

This past year has been absolutely amazing and wonderful in various aspects and a painful one on many levels as well. Almost every month, something significant happened that changed my life. Yet, I look at my resilience in overcoming and the happiness I still have through it all. When I look at the pain of this past year, I realize most of it was caused by the actions of others which impacted my life by choices they made that affected me. Of course, there are parts of the pain that I also created within myself. Rather than choosing to play the victim, I took the initiative to gain real healing and empower myself.

I think back to a year ago and recognize how different my life is today because I was willing to invest in myself and in my own healing. Today I am a completely different person. I think of all the life changing effects on my own life using energy healing and essential oils and stand in awe of what has taken place since writing the first book. I have experienced my marriage literally transform into what I've always wanted it to be. My relationship with self and my business has been transformational as well.

As I have participated in energy work being performed on me on a regular basis, I have felt lighter, my confidence in myself has grown, and so has my belief in self. I have been able to let go of old patterns and cycles in the past that held me back. I feel joy and such a peace that at times is indescribable. It's a place I never want to leave.

I'm even more amazed at the transformation within me over the past 10 years. God led me on this journey to find myself, and through serving others, I found healing within. I'm at a place in life where I KNOW my purpose and I know what I came here to do and every morning I wake up excited about what I get to do every day. This was not my life 10 years ago. Sometimes our mess turns into our message. My life 10 years ago does not even resemble what it is today. I was experiencing a horrible divorce, became mom and dad 24/7 to three young boys, and found myself homeless and moving to another city to have a roof over our heads. I thought my life was over, but little did I know it was just beginning. I had lost any belief in myself and I was in a dark place. I felt alone and full of questions. Little by little, I learned to believe in myself again. Over time, healing entered my heart and light grew within me to dissipate the darkness and I have never been the same.

Before the healing light came, though, there was that point in my life that I was really a miserable person. I compared myself to everyone and I thought life was all about what fate dealt you. I was just existing and 'trying' to be better and yet I complained A LOT so I judged myself and others harshly. I criticized others and myself often. I thought that I wasn't deserving of happiness. Betrayal on every level reared its ugly head. I questioned everything I thought I knew and I doubted myself completely. I lost trust in myself and others.

As I experienced divorce, I became clinically depressed and literally prayed to die! I clearly remember kneeling in my closet crying and begging and pleading with the Lord to take me. The pain was so unbearable that there were days I cried and could hardly breathe. Everything I believed in was shattered and I felt so broken, like my heart was crumbling into a million pieces, never to be put back together again. I had three young boys to care for, and I was praying to die! That's how low I was feeling in the dark place I existed in. I thought my life was over because it didn't go the way I had planned for it to be. I had experienced abuse on all levels and I felt I had done everything in my power for life to be different and better. Yet I was still in my own prison and didn't even know how stuck I really was. I was a prisoner to my own thoughts and beliefs. At the time, I didn't know any different. I was doing the best I could with what I knew.

I pushed through and tried to overcome and finally immersed myself in self development books to try and "fix all my brokenness." I was saying affirmations over and over, trying so hard to CONVINCE myself that I was rich or happy or successful, and honestly, it worked for me...for a little while...Now, I'm not knocking self development at all, I totally believe in it and I still read books daily because I find great value in them and gain much insight, BUT it wasn't until I finally got to the core of healing myself that I started getting HUGE results in my life, where I FELT successful and happy and abundant! There is quite a difference in convincing ourselves, as opposed to actually and finally feeling it. I'm a totally different person than I was back then and I continue to expand and grow and evolve. I know that even a year from now I will be different than who I am today. Thank goodness God had a totally different plan for me than the one I was on. He saw greater things in me than I could have ever imagined. I had been playing small for years and, honestly, I think He felt it was time to yank me out of it and to create the life I really signed up for. Those rocks were thick and heavy and it was quite the journey to remove them to finally see my light within.

I knew that God was up-leveling my life because I wasn't getting to where I needed to be.

Ann Webb (Founder of My Ideal Life Vision) said it so eloquently:

When it's time to up-level your life, be prepared for what has been called "the dark night of the soul."

Your friends and family don't understand what you're going through (unless they have experienced their own DARK NIGHT).

-Whatever compassion is offered can't even begin to reach the depth of your despair.

-The path you're following has become dry as dust and clearly isn't working anymore.

-You start wondering that maybe God isn't real after all and transformation can NEVER be worth this!

-You question your worthiness and your words.

-You feel completely alone and betrayed.

-Agonizing emotions convince you that you are not going to survive the hopeless state of being, and that you might die- and if you did- well that would be perfectly ok.

-It's more than sadness, depression or anxiety.

-It's called the dark night of the soul because you wonder "how do I make it through the night?"

-You cry everyday.

And yet…

-You find out that every wise and enlightened person has gone through it.

-It's inescapable, and actually desirable because it's the transforming touch of the Spirit.

-You learn that the endurance of darkness is preparation for greater light.

-You learn that you're strong, and that the spiritual benefits of embracing it might be worth the grueling pain.

-You go to bed thinking you know something and wake up saying, "I DON'T KNOW ANYTHING!"

-Your ego gives way to spirit and that's beautiful (a bad day for the ego is a good day for the soul).

-It's your refiner's fire—your Gethsemane

If you have made a commitment to God and yourself that you're ready to evolve and awaken—be prepared!

The "Dark Night of the Soul" puts an end to your life as you know it, including the parts you wish would never change. But when you are serious to up-leveling spiritually, God will crush your ego and my advice is simply HEED. Just surrender. It's going to be ugly and hurt like HELL, but at the end of the day, week or even year, you are like the butterfly emerging from the chrysalis. Trust God. Thank God.   Ann Webb

The "Dark Night of the Soul" I experienced nearly knocked me under but in the end it became the beginning of a huge purging my spirit needed to experience to get to the next level that would catapult me into the growth my spirit was crying out for so that change could finally happen.

Even through the darkness I was experiencing, I made a commitment to myself to never again get into a relationship where I handed my power over and allowed someone to abuse me physically and/or emotionally. I knew I had great healing to do within myself before I could even think of being in another relationship, so I allowed myself the time I needed to heal. I went to the depths of humility and I took ownership of my own actions and my own dysfunctionality that I had created in my relationship. I had to do some hard core soul searching and overcoming and letting go. I had to forgive others and forgive myself. I had to choose love instead of hate and bitterness. I had to finally choose freedom.

The thing is it was a LOOOOOOOOONNGGG road to get there and I wish I had someone who had shown me the shortcuts because I now know that there was a quicker and more effective way to heal than what I was doing. So today that is what I teach and practice and the results have been amazing for many.

Today I have an amazing husband who is my partner and best friend and we have created a great marriage. We have an incredible family of wonderful children after being a single mom for 8 years. I have several successful businesses and I get to travel the country, but do you know what? Even those things don't define who I am.

I have found a deep, meaningful and more permanent healing and purpose in who I am and what I came here to do. I decided I am worth loving and I have an amazing life full of joy! This makes me a better mother, wife, sister and friend.

But my story doesn't stop there. Even after I remarried and had already found so much healing, I had several experiences that yet again knocked me over the head and shook my foundation to the very core, including another "Dark Night of the Soul" experience. It wiped me out.

What I knew and believed in wasn't truth and I saw betrayal at the deepest level. I went through a painful experience as one lie after another unfolded about what I had believed in for the previous 20 years of my life and even into my childhood. It was devastating and painful and overwhelming to the point that my body shut down. I literally laid in bed one day where I couldn't even move my head or hands to drink a cup of water. I couldn't eat or even make sense of my thoughts. My heart was once again shattered and broken and I felt lost. I felt anguish. Anger welled up inside of me as I tried to process all that I was experiencing and all the raw emotion that felt so overwhelming and all consuming. Again, pain took my breath away. I experienced many forms of betrayal and a questioning of the whole foundation I grew up on. Though I wasn't angry at God, I questioned Him and how this could all be happening and why?

But this time, because I had tools I didn't have before, the healing took place at a deeper level and in a more efficient and effective way. I had insight. I had experience. I had growth, and I had powerful knowledge that helped to create healing at an accelerated level without having to relive the drama or the trauma. This time, rather than years, it took weeks to overcome and it was powerful. Instead of resisting, I went in full force and walked through it and overcame while God showed me the miracles of healing that could really take place within me. I had energy healing and the power of essential oils on my side and it was a whole new dimension of healing than ever before. The extent of forgiveness I had to find within me was greater than I had ever experienced before. I had to draw from a well deep within to let go of the pain and emotions that came about from the consequences I was paying because of the choices of significant people in my life. Alas, I also had to find the greatest healing within and forgive myself as well. I find this to be one of the greatest obstacles my clients have is forgiveness of self. I think we all struggle to overcome that at some point in our lives. That's why I want to share everything with you; to make your journey more vibrant and your healing more efficient and powerful and permanent. I'm confident it will raise you to a level you've never known before and can benefit you now and forever.

Because of my own healing experiences and the tools I've used, I've shared them with many. Some have shared the essential oils and observed others using them in their own professions and have seen positive results. We know of counselors using them in their practice who saw clients opening up more in sessions and revealing more feelings than they had previously, just because of diffusing oils in their office. I have seen more progress in my own clients. I feel like they have a tool to empower themselves. I had a client who was having a meltdown and a difficult time getting to sleep and letting go of many random thoughts in her head. She used a blend of essential oils and an immediate calm overcame her. The oils helped tremendously in gathering her thoughts and emotions to better handle herself.

When my youngest son moved out to live in a foreign country for two years, although I felt joy that he was fulfilling a dream, it was a huge transition in my life and I felt a sadness overtake me, I used a blend of oils and was struck by the peace that came over me as I breathed them in using a diffuser. My sleep was more restful and my nervousness and anxiousness went away.

I had a client who had deep seeded anger issues and was about to lose his job over it. He was told he had to get his anger under control or his franchise would be taken from him. After several sessions with me and the use of essential oils he was able to gain control of his anger. In his own words, he said, "I literally feel like I'm in a whole new body. The tension and anger is no longer there and I now laugh at things that used to make me so angry in a matter of seconds. I feel like a completely different person." We have countless stories like these that have been transformational experiences for many as they have used these powerful tools.

Karisa's Story

When we look upon our day to day life, often it seems as though we are stuck. I know I have felt this. The past year has been one of amazing experiences, but also one of digging deep, enduring and learning through tough 'life curriculum,' and growing to new heights and in ways I can't express.

This book is going to be real, raw, and contain our experiences that are personal and meaningful. Ones that, to be honest, scare us a little as we 'share' our vulnerability and allow the world in on our own hard times and lives. There is a reason we are doing this though. One, I know that there are many out there who will be able to relate; who will be able to share tears with me as they too personally know the pangs of heartache and tenderness that these experiences carry. Most importantly, we share because there are tools that help to heal, overcome, endure, and grow magnificently. That is what the purpose of this book is- to share in the beautiful growth, to teach tools to endure in happiness and joy, and to transform into spiritual lights that give love and shine brightly.

My last year has been amazing in many ways. I've been to the other side of the world and experienced beautiful and transformational personal healing. I also got the chance to travel back and forth across the United States teaching and mentoring. I moved into a big beautiful home on Long Island, received amazing leadership roles in personally significant women's organizations, and served with a tireless heart.

In the same year, however, I have also experienced my greatest heartaches yet. I have felt the heavy weight of various responsibilities. The real physical strain of being pulled in multiple roles and positions. The tiring and life-sucking results of living a life unbalanced. I have had great doubts about my own self-worth and beauty, felt stuck in my business and life, cried from the impact and actions of others, and felt torn, worn down, and real, honest heartbreak. Words cut deep sometimes and the actions of others do affect us, too. Our self-talk limits or liberates us. These things are all real.

I have learned much through these great lessons. These are all experiences we face that allow us the opportunity to grow. We all have the choice in regards to how we will react, what we will do, and how we allow each experience to mold and shape us. I call this our 'life curriculum'. The last three years, I think I've been in some of the 'advanced courses' in regards to personal relationships and unconditional love. What a great blessing to look back though and see what has evolved, blossomed, and grown as a result.

A couple of these tools we share and teach in this book were spiritually gifted to me in those moments of heartache and even in moments of hard-heartedness (aka stubbornness). They brought light, healing, comfort, and peace. They came with special experiences of profound love and light. The essential oils magnified the healing effect and the results associated. It was beautiful. These were moments when, once again, I learned that this life is about more than just my little bubble in the world and the impact and ripple effect I can have and will bring to the world one person at a time as I share and spread to others can be powerful.

***

So, how does this all work? Is there really any science behind it? Why do essential oils and energy healing work so well together and how do they really accelerate your healing? You're about to find out as we explain all of this to you in the following chapters, and once again provide you healing tools to practice on yourself and others.

Energy & Vibration

Everything around us is filled with and comprised of energy. When we inhale molecules, those molecules trigger electrical signals that are sent to our brain and processed as scents. Everything carries an energy to it. Even our words, thoughts, and atmosphere carry an energy that can affect not only us, but those around us. In addition, those we are around affect us.

Energy Effects Matter

This energy can either be beneficial or non-beneficial. There is no neutral, un-effective energy. Everything has an impact on us, even if it is mild. Our personal experiences, treatment from others, environment, nutrition we consume, etc. It all has an energy that affects us either beneficially or non-beneficially.

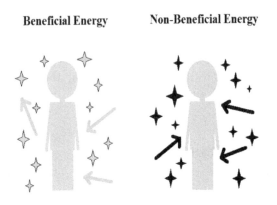

Beneficial Energy   **Non-Beneficial Energy**

Do you ever find yourself in a situation where you are around someone who is negative, who complains a lot, is rude, or just heavy hearted? If you are a very positive person, this may cause some discomfort, or you may not want to be around this other person. You may even find that you too may get into a low mood or even just feel tired or drained after spending time around them.

Non-beneficial energy could even be from a negative or traumatic experience. For example, one may have experienced a traumatic loss at a very young age. When something like that happens at such a young age, a child typically doesn't have the proper understanding or tools to process that experience entirely, so it gets shoved down deeper and deeper within. It then is 'stuck' and can surface or affect their emotional reactions.

Non-Beneficial Energy Can Get Stuck

What is needed is a way to process and release that blocked non-beneficial energy and then replace that space with positive, beneficial energy. This will create healing and a space for positive energy with a higher frequency and vibration which is what the body and spirit needs in order to achieve different results and let go of stuck non-beneficial energy.

That is where essential oils and energy work both come into play. They are both tools that can be used to remove non-beneficial energy and implement beneficial energy. When combined together, the healing power is magnified.

A visual example of the power of combining tools, like essential oils with energy, can be seen easily an example using sunlight and water. First, both water and sunlight are powerfully healing and beneficial. If you were to look at water droplets, maybe morning dew for example, you would see that alone, they are beautiful. Water provides nutrients for the plants, animals, and even ourselves. Now, take the sunlight. It provides warmth, healing, comfort, and even nutrients to the plants and ourselves as well. When that sunlight shines bright and right into the water droplet, that light is magnified. The water droplet looks like a diamond with light refracting in many directions. It is beautiful. The sunlight represents energy and the water droplet represents the tools that we can use. The tools used in this book combine energy work with essential oils. They are literally a tool of light and a healing liquid.

Vibration and Frequency

"Everything in life is a vibration"- Albert Einstein

Since everything is energy, it also has a vibration that can be measured through its frequency. Frequency shows the value of the energy being represented. We are energetic beings. Our bodies have energy and what we put on or take into our body also has an energy. The food that we eat has an energy. There is a vibration to everything within and around us and we are affected by it either positively or negatively. When we recognize this, we can then focus on what may be beneficial to our body that can actually increase the positive energy within us and literally increase our vibration.

We included these charts in our first book and talked about frequency and vibration. Everything is energy and therefore everything has a frequency.

These are charts that show the frequency of our body at different stages.

Frequency of People and Things	MHz
Human Brain	72-90 MHz
Human Body (Day)	62-68 MHz
Cold Symptoms	58 MHz
Flu Symptoms	57 MHz
Candida	55 MHz
Epstein-Barr	52 MHz
Cancer	42 MHz
Onset of Death	25 MHz
Processed Canned Food	0 MHz
Fresh Produce	Up to 15MHz
Dry Herbs	12-22 MHz
Fresh Herbs	20-27 MHz
Essential Oils	52-320 MHz

Frequency of People and Things Data from the Reference Guide to Essential Oils by C&A Higley

As you notice, the more disease and illness set into our bodies, the lower the vibration goes. Physical ailments decrease the body's vibration and are usually manifested from something emotional within the body. The onset of cancer lowers the vibration of the body significantly. When emotions aren't processed within the body, the emotions get stuck within the body. For instance, imagine feeling angry at the age of 6 that you weren't picked to play on a team at recess. Your feelings were hurt and you were embarrassed but you didn't want anyone to know so you didn't show it and you pushed it down instead of really feeling it and processing it. The low vibration energy from this emotion has to go somewhere when it isn't fully processed so it makes a home within your body until it can be released.

Our thoughts also carry a frequency to them. The thoughts we believe are powerful and the beliefs we take in have an energy and vibration to them as well.

In the book *Man Triumphant*, Annalee Skarin shares this: (page 66)

"The power of controlling one's vibrations, when comprehended, is one of the most simple procedures in existence. It is the road Christ travelled. It is the road of power when one travels it knowingly. One's dynamic powers of creation can be mis-used or abused or they can be used with unlimited power for good. One's vibrations can be weak, nil and almost non-existent. Or they can be repulsive. It is always up to the individual to select the caliber of his released vibrations as he sends them out under control."

"One must truly comprehend the stupendous energy released with every dynamic thought and feeling."

"Every caliber of thought has its own vibrations. Every word, every emotion contains dynamic potency and must, of its own nature, release the vibrations which pertain to it. No one can think, or feel, or speak without sending out the vibrations he creates with his released thoughts and words and feelings and actions. These vibrations he releases are his own creation. Vibrations are released with every thought and feeling whether the creator is aware of what he is doing or not."[1]

That last line is very powerful! Vibrations are released with every thought and feeling we have! When you continue to add emotions that aren't fully processed, over time, there is a lot of low vibration energy in your body and as it festers, it starts to cause physical ailments, like stomach problems or diseases, etc.

As you look at the chart, you can see why disease can set in when your frequency and vibration is lowered by these low vibration emotions. As you notice in the next chart, the essential oils are actually high vibration. Many have higher frequencies than the body at a normal healthy range.

Frequency of Single Essential Oils	MHz	
Rose	320	MHz
Helichrysum	181	MHz
Frankincense	147	MHz
Ravensara	134	MHz
Lavender	118	MHz
German Chamomile	105	MHz
Idaho Tansy	105	MHz
Myrrh	105	MHz
Melissa	102	MHz
Juniper	98	MHz
Sandalwood	96	MHz
Angelica	85	MHz
Peppermint	78	MHz
Galbanum	56	MHz
Basil	52	MHz

Frequency of Essential Oils Data from the Reference Guide to Essential Oils by C&A Higley

High vibration cannot exist in a low vibration environment and vice versa. As you apply a high frequency oil to your body, you literally increase the frequency and vibration of your body, therefore creating a space to release low vibration emotions that can no longer exist in a high vibration environment. That's how the power of these oils can benefit the body emotionally. There is of course a science behind it but it really can be explained that simply.

How Scents Affect Our Memory and Emotions

How Our Olfactory System Works

Our bodies are so beautifully and divinely designed. Every part of our being is designed to support us in our journey in mortality.

The earth is a beautiful gift that contains everything within it that we need to heal ourselves. Essential oils truly are a powerful gift from the earth for this purpose physically, emotionally, and spiritually. We are not only affecting ourselves as we experience the healing process, but we are affecting all the energy around us, and the individuals as well.

To dive a little deeper into how the essential oils work physically with the body to promote and cause emotional healing, we must first review the parts of the body that are involved.

To better understand the relationship between scents, emotions, and memories, first one must know the olfactory system and its components. To begin, when we inhale particles or molecules of a specific scent, there is a path it follows and a powerhouse destination, the amygdala, where it is processed.

The path it follows begins in the nasal cavity where scent molecules are absorbed by epithelial olfactory cells that line the inner cavity of our nose. The olfactory cells within this olfactory epithelium are nerve cells that are especially designed with cilia, small hair-like structures that extend into the nasal cavity. There are one to five million of these cells with numerous cilia attached in each side of the nose. The cilia each have receptors that bind to a specific type of odor molecule.

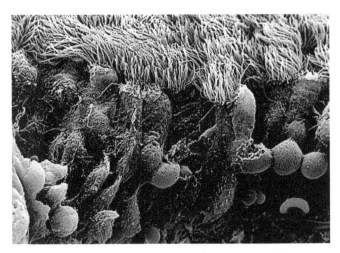

Photo credit: www.greathillsent.com

When we recognize a specific scent, it is because of the combination of those specific variations of molecules that create that scent response. For example, a 'coffee' smell or odor is a combination of over 100 different scent molecules.[2]

These molecules send a signal, or information, that then travels up to the olfactory bulb. This is where the coding of the information is processed. This information, once decoded, then travels along the lateral olfactory tract to the amygdala.

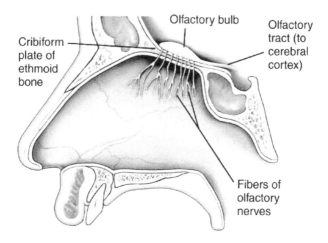

Photo credit: Olfactory Nerve to Brain, The Free Dictionary

The amygdala is part of the limbic system that is very important to one's being, personality behaviors, reactions, and memories. The amygdala is responsible for memory, decision-making, and emotions or emotional reactions and the only way to stimulate the amygdala is via the olfactory system and the sense of smell.

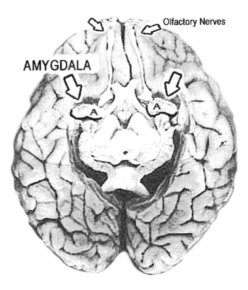

AMYGDALA

Olfactory Nerves

There are two amygdalae, one on each hemisphere or side of our brain. There is one on the left and one on the right. Each side actually has been found to respond differently to stimuli as well. In one study done in 2007[3], it was found that when the right amygdala was stimulated, it induced negative emotions such as fear and sadness. Thus, the right amygdala is associated with negative emotions. When the left amygdala was stimulated, it was able to induce either pleasant emotions such as happiness, or negative emotions such as fear, anxiety, and sadness.

Therefore, the left was able to react to both positive and aversive emotions, whereas the right only reacted to aversive emotions. This shows how essential positive emotions are and how damaging the negative thoughts can be. Our brain literally has twice the capacity to react to the negative emotions, or half the ability to process the good ones.

The amygdala's primary role is in the "formation and storage of memories associated with emotional events."[4] When an event or experience has powerful emotions tied to it, that memory can have a stronger impact on a future reaction or response or even on the ability to recall that memory. Response emotions are therefore attached to the memory stimuli. An example of this could be someone who has experienced a car crash which results in a fear of driving or even being a passenger in a car. The emotion of fear at the traumatic crash attached itself to the stimuli of driving or being driven. This attachment then results in a fear response simply by driving or being in a car. Another example could be a child who experiences the loss of a parent. The intense sadness, loss, loneliness, emptiness, or even confusion that the child feels ties itself to the withdrawal of the parental care-figure. This child, once older, may experience these feelings surface again with a change in a personal relationship, causing the resulting emotions from that change in relationship to be exacerbated.

When given tools and knowledge about how to change, support, and clear the initial negative emotional response to past experiences or situations, you are, in a way, able to reprogram the brain to store the memory and emotional response in a different, maybe even positive way.

Christi had an experience that is a beautiful example of how adjusting and clearing the emotional response from a traumatic or negative event as soon as possible can limit the non-beneficial energy that is stored from it, and also limit the emotional response attached to the memory. Here is her experience in her own words:

"I had an intense experience this year that shows a perfect example of what we have just explained. I had flown to California from Texas to teach some classes on essential oils and to do some live healing sessions. The day started off amazingly beautiful! Honestly, the weather and the company could not have been more perfect. We were driven from the airport to a beautiful restaurant overlooking the water where I had an enjoyable lunch that came with great conversation, laughter and tantalizing food.

"We then drove to a friend's home. She lived in a magnificent upscale neighborhood in Camarillo, California. This was a neighborhood with multimillion dollar homes with gorgeous landscaping and we drove into her tree-lined driveway. I was relaxed and full of joy, anticipating seeing her beautiful gardens. There were three of us in the car and our wonderful hostess proceeded to open her door and get out of the car and go into her garage to gather her cats inside.

"As soon as the garage door closed we noticed two men walking up her driveway to our car. My friend sat in the front and I sat in the back. I all of a sudden had a foreboding feeling something was really off. Unbeknownst to us, a car had followed us into the neighborhood with an agenda of their own, waiting for us to pull into the driveway. A man lunged into the front seat and held a gun to my friend as another man lunged into the back seat at me and pointed a gun to my side. In an instant, everything seemed to become slow motion and a million thoughts ran through my mind. I felt helpless because I felt so limited by what I could do and still be safe. I was on high alert because my life was being threatened if I didn't do what was asked of me. Adrenaline was pumping through my body. I was stunned silent. We were told to give them everything we had. I think the shock of it all was not quite registering because we were thrown so off guard. My friend actually asked if they were serious, to which the response was to point the guns at our head. I felt as though my spirit was almost leaving my body because it was too much to handle at once. I literally thought I might be living the last seconds of my life. It is a surreal moment to look down the barrel of a gun inches away and pointed straight at you. Something startled them and they grabbed our purses and our phones and ran. Later we were to find that they were LA gang members. As soon as they left, survivor instinct kicked in and I was in fast motion to get us some help. I called the police and was able to recall in detail what happened but as soon as I got on the phone with my husband, the emotions overcame me and the tears started flowing. He couldn't even understand what I was saying because at that point, all emotions took over. My friend experienced the same thing. We were shaken up and rightly so. Our bodies were in shock from the events.

"The very next day, my friend and I started the processes to release emotions through energy healing and immediately started to apply essential oils. During the threat we weren't able to release the emotions coming up inside of us and so we took this opportunity to identify and release them immediately rather than getting stuck somewhere in our body. Remarkably enough, we were still able to accomplish all we had come there to do with teaching classes and doing sessions for the remainder of the trip, despite having had such a traumatic experience, and did not shut down from fear and overwhelm. Still to this day, I see the extremely positive benefits of the work we did on ourselves, as neither of us feel any overwhelm at the memory of this very traumatic experience in our lives."

Christi's traumatic experience didn't limit the ability to complete her tasks or enjoy the remainder of her trip, because she was able to begin the process to release the emotional response attached to her experience immediately.

By implementing essential oils to calm her reaction and emotions, she was able to physically and emotionally impact her response that would have been stored otherwise. Therefore, her reactions and emotions to stimuli that trigger this memory were, and will be, more controlled and realistic versus an exaggerated or excessive response.

Our olfactory system is more powerful and complex than neuroscientists have yet been able to fully discover. In recent years, scientists have discovered our body has scent receptors not just in our nose, but literally all over our body. They are in our muscle tissue, kidneys, in blood vessels, in the skin, in heart tissue, and more. These scent or chemical receptors in other areas of our body send signals and information to our brain, but don't necessarily process it as a scent. Our body is capable of processing chemical signals via olfactory receptors all over our body. Scientists are continually learning more and more about the olfactory system. Stunningly, there are more genes devoted to decoding odor information than are devoted to any other function in our body or brain by a factor of at least twenty. That is a powerful and eye-opening statement to the power of the olfactory system.

As mentioned before, our amygdala and olfactory system can only be triggered by scent. In addition, essential oils have distinct properties that allow them to trigger different responses in the brain.

"Because the limbic system is directly connected to those parts of the brain that control heart rate, blood pressure, breathing, memory, stress levels, and hormone balance, essential oils can have profound physiological and psychological effects... Olfactory responses to odors induce the brain to stimulate the release of hormones and neurochemicals that in turn alter the body's physiology and behavior."
-Essential Oil Desk Reference, 4th Edition

Scent molecules work as a code to trigger different responses when they are 'keyed' into the olfactory receptors. Some molecules and scents help to calm and others may stimulate, for example. In order to do these things, the signals given by these molecules actually trigger the brain to release hormones to cause the correlating responses. It is a beautiful domino effect. Scent molecules and essential oils can initiate a response and even change the nervous system biochemistry.

"A Japanese study found that inhaling essential oils can modulate your sympathetic nervous system activity. Certain oils were found to be stimulating, while others were found to be calming. For example:

- Black pepper, fennel, and grapefruit oil caused a 1.5-to 2.5-fold increase in sympathetic nervous system activity (as measured by an increase in systolic blood pressure).
- Rose and patchouli oil resulted in a 40 percent decrease in sympathetic nervous system activity.
- Pepper oil induced a 1.7-fold increase in plasma adrenaline concentration, while rose oil caused adrenaline to drop by 30 percent.
- Other oils have been shown to measurably decrease stress hormones—inhaling lavender and rosemary were shown to reduce cortisol levels.

As mentioned earlier, scents play a powerful role in memories, especially emotional memories."[5]

As you can see, there are some types of oils that have calming responses while others have stimulating responses. Different types of scent molecules trigger different emotional reactions. All essential oils are composed of different volatile aromatic compounds.[6] Mint essential oils have alcohol and ketones that are energizing and calming. Citrus essential oils have monoterpenes which are uplifting and revitalizing. Spice essential oils have ethers and esters which are renewing and intriguing. Herbs and grasses have phenols which are comforting and soothing. Trees and woods have alcohols which are grounding and balancing. Florals have esters which are calming and reassuring. This is why essential oils can promote strong emotional responses.

When it comes to the physical response and emotional response that is benefitted from an essential oil, they are correlated and connected in what they help to do. For instance, Jasmine is an essential oil that is physically stimulating and arousing. Emotionally it uplifts mood and is an oil that aids in sexual healing. Frankincense is able to pass through the blood brain barrier and affect the brain physically, aid in cellular restoration, mood balance, and so much more. The blood brain barrier protects the brain and is one of the most selective filtering systems in the body. Emotionally, Frankincense is also able to encourage a high level of energetic filtration as it is an oil that promotes divine light or truth, which draws one closer to divinity and the grandeur of the True Self. Another example is Geranium, physically it supports the circulatory system and the heart. Emotionally it is an oil that opens the heart more to accept love and encourages trust; opening the heart to receive love, forgiveness, and acceptance. All of the essential oils emotionally correspond to their physical benefits. We have these olfactory receptors all over inside our body, receiving these chemical signals. This is one reason why we can apply an essential oil to the bottom of our feet, allowing it to be absorbed into the bloodstream, so that we are able to benefit systemically. These olfactory receptors send the electrical stimuli back to the nervous system, even if it is not processed as a smell, just as do the receptors triggering the physical response.

The combinations or blends of essential oils, just like with the example of coffee, have a different 'scent' that is decoded and encourages different emotional benefits. It can be more powerful as these individual oils combine and become one high vibrational scent. They can address a whole array of emotions because, rather than just one scent, there is a beautiful combination of oils. Blends are useful when addressing an array of emotions in a single situation. Whereas, when a specific emotion is ready to be processed, that corresponding oil can be more beneficial in addressing that specific emotion.

Implementing a grouping or order of individual oils, one after the next, can enhance the process of emotional healing as it releases the layers of a specific area or emotion in your life. That's how energy healing works. Things are released layer by layer. It is a continual and ongoing process of cleansing and healing. I want to re-emphasize the importance of learning and understanding that. Emotional healing is a continual process of development, growth, progression, and understanding. As we heal in one area of our lives, we are able to uncover where else we can heal and grow. It is a process that is continual and on-going, as humans by nature are ever-changing and experiencing new things daily. Even great examples of peace and love in history, like Mother Teresa and Gandhi, devoted their entire lives to growing in these areas.

Our bodies are absolutely phenomenal and profound miracles. As already mentioned, there are more genes devoted to decoding odor information than are devoted to any other function in our body or brain by a factor of at least twenty. That emphasizes the impact that these molecules can have on not only our olfactory system, but our entire body, in ways we still have yet to discover and understand. When combining energy work and applying essential oils immediately upon experiencing a traumatic experience, or when implementing healing techniques to past experiences, it provides a powerful cleansing experience that can be effective systemically.

Due to the ties and connection between memory and emotion initiated in the amygdala, treating traumatic or deeply emotional experiences immediately can transform the memory stored from an aversive experience to a positive one so that the negative emotional reaction is healed or cleared. Clearing the non-beneficial emotions and reaction immediately helps the memory so it is not stored as a negative one. This allows your memory, whether conscious or subconscious, to not have a negative effect on your life until you are mature or able to address it through other tools such as those described in this book. When powerful emotional experiences are addressed immediately, we have enhanced the ability to control our response and reaction. When we master control over our output and intake, we've mastered what we allow to affect us, how we respond, and therefore the quality of our lives. Even just using an oil when you've had a powerful emotional experience and consciously releasing the negative emotions can have a powerful response energetically.

The tools in this book are designed to address past issues that were not able to be addressed immediately due to lack of tools, knowledge, or information at the time.

Intuition

What is it?

It has been said that "prayer is your phone line to God and intuition is God's phone line to you." Intuition is your inner wisdom in its truest form. You have many answers within you and fine tuning your intuition cultivates the wisdom within. Strengthening your intuition can truly be one of the most powerful tools you have! In my line of work, it is key to what I do.

Have you ever had an experience where you had the thought "Hmmmm...maybe I shouldn't do this"? And you did it anyway and you ended up regretting that you went ahead even though your gut told you not to? That was your intuition at work and guess what? It's right 100% of the time.

As kids, we tend to listen and to be more open to our intuition. But as adults, we tend to question it a great deal. Our intuition is our truth. It is that moment when we feel something is off, it's that feeling when we feel our passion and purpose, or it's when we know something is about to happen. Intuition is the truth of who you are to your core. It's that inner voice or inner knowing that has your own answers.

When I was in my first marriage, I felt a powerful intuitive prompting one day to buy tickets for our family to go visit my husband's mother in Florida. I felt strongly that we were to do this, though I didn't know why. It just felt urgent and important. The only other trip we had taken to see her was a few years prior and we drove. After that, she came to visit us. I received this intuitive prompting several times and shared it with my husband. Normally, he would have had a difficult time getting the time off work during the holiday it fell on, but one thing after another fell into place in order for us to go, so we did. We were able to get some great deals on airline tickets. We flew out to see her and had a great time, made some great memories together, and she was able to visit with her grandchildren. A few months later she became very ill and suddenly passed away. We wouldn't have seen her before she passed had I not acted on this and followed through. I was grateful I had listened to my intuition.

Sometimes we allow negativity to cloud our intuition and push it down, choosing to listen to our ego or other people over own inner voice. If we allow it to guide us, our inner voice has so much wisdom and insight for us to learn from. Why are we so quick to listen to everyone else or to the negativity within ourselves, rather than the voice we should trust the most?

I was facilitating a workshop one day and I divided the group into several small groups. I had one person stand on a chair and a person next to them stand on a chair, then I had people circle around the two on the chair. Participant 1 on the chair was the person who was to speak their truth and their dreams to the world and voice their heart's desire. Participant 2 on the chair next to them was to be their intuition and voice of positivity, their "higher self", the truth and encouragement. The people on the ground around them in a circle were to be the "nay sayers" and their job was to tell them every reason they were not going to succeed at the very dream participant 1 was expressing. They were to tell them all the things our ego and others tell us when we have dreams and get discouraged and knocked down, all those things we say to ourselves or others say to us. During this exercise, one of the women on the floor- a "nay sayer" became very emotional and started to cry. She expressed how bad she felt telling someone else they couldn't live their dream and knocking them down. It was painful for her to do that to someone else. I asked her this question, "How is it any different than what you say to yourself every day in your own negative self-doubting talk in your head, or when you talk yourself out of doing something your intuition is telling you to take the risk to do?" It took her back for a second as she realized she found it easier to say these negative things to herself, sometimes even on a daily basis, rather than to say it to someone else. Why have we gotten so used to such negative self talk? Why aren't we listening to our truth and intuition more? Why are we listening to our ego more?

How do you strengthen your intuition? Great question! Intuition is an inner knowing. When you ask yourself a question, usually, if in the first 3 seconds you get an answer, that is your intuition speaking. After 3 seconds, it is usually your ego. It is a real battle sometimes to overcome the thoughts of your ego. Your ego can be a real killer to intuitive thoughts and feelings. It tends to make you want to question what your intuition is telling you. It takes courage to silence the ego and allow your intuition to be your voice and center stage to your life. Strengthening your intuition can help you in overcoming your ego and negative self-talk.

Ways to strengthen your intuition:

Meditation - Quieting your mind so that you can get more in touch with yourself and your intuition can be powerful in strengthening it. Get quiet within yourself. This allows space for you to start listening to yourself more, rather than to everything and everyone around you. Meditation is a key to strengthening you intuition as you tune into you.

Listen to your Gut - Your gut has a myriad of emotions that can be felt within and there are neurotransmitters that can signal to you physically what is going on inside your gut. Our gut is our second brain and it can tell us a lot about our feelings because we carry a lot of emotion in it. Next time you try to get in touch with what it feels like in your gut, ask yourself if you feel queasy or anxious or fearful? Maybe it's trying to tell you something.

Develop the Gift of Listening To Your Intuition Through Writing - A book that was life changing for me was "Writing Down Your Soul" by Janet Conner. I have always been one to journal most of my life, but the way journaling was presented in this book was different than what I had ever done before. It strengthened my intuition like nothing else and I would encourage you to get the book for yourself because it is so insightful and powerful in strengthening your intuition. Basically, in simple terms, I learned to sit and write "Dear Voice," at the top of my journal page each morning and then I would proceed to write all that was weighing on my heart that day. I would pour my heart out and, in my writings, I would ask questions. Pretty soon I started to hear a voice within me respond with the answers. It became easier and easier for me to find the answers to the questions I was seeking and more like a conversation in my head between me and my spirit. It was amazing how strong my intuition grew from this. Writing is a powerful tool in getting in tune to yourself and your intuition.

Start trusting yourself - The more you doubt and question yourself, the weaker your intuition becomes. If you mess up, move forward and learn from it but do not let it keep you from finding the answers within. Trust your voice and your inner knowing. When people are following the voice of true intuition they describe themselves as feeling the following:

- a sense of connection or belonging
- openness
- lack of doubt
- clarity
- relaxation
- surprise
- awe
- joy
- excitement
- fulfillment
- inspiration
- brightness

Trusting yourself is key to strengthening your intuition.

The dancer, Agnes de Mille, once said, "Bodies never lie. Like an exquisite tuning fork, your intuitive body will tell you the truth. You can learn its language and know to trust it."

Our body knows what it needs, our spirit knows the answers, our heart knows its truth. All this requires us being in tune to our intuition. When we are in tuned to our intuition it can help us meet the needs of our body, mind, and soul.

Using Your Intuition with Essential Oils

Our bodies are designed with a beautiful way of knowing exactly what they need when they need it. When we need sleep, we become tired. When we are hungry, we know we need to fuel our body. Often, we can know what nutrients our body needs by the foods we crave. An obvious example of this is when we are thirsty, we need water. A more subtle signal might be when we are in need of something like iron, we may crave iron rich foods like red meats.

When we are in tune with our body, we can determine what our body's signals are trying to tell us. We can determine what it needs to bring its functioning level to its maximum potential.

We can experience this when using and implementing essential oils as well. I'll share a quick story as an example of this.

When I was first starting to use essential oils, I was gifted a calming blend of essential oils that I absolutely loved. I saw that it was for calming and knew that I could benefit from it. I was going through a very trying time in my family life where I was being stretched and strained and was under more stress than usual. So, this oil spoke to me and I craved to use it multiple times a day. After time and consistent use of the blend, I found that it no longer drew the appeal it once had. I was slightly confused by this because the stressor was still present in my life. I felt prompted to return once again to my "treasure box of oils", as I like to call it, to determine which oil would then become my favorite. The next oil I was drawn to was one that had a scent that, to me personally, had carried a repulsive smell the first time I'd opened the bottle. I decided to give it a try and opened in again. Now, although the scent wasn't my favorite, I found myself drawn to it and wanted to continue smelling it.

There had been a change.

Emotionally, my body was not ready for the healing the second, stronger smelling oil provided when I experienced it the first time. At that time, I was ready for the calming blend. My body was prepared and ready to process and address the emotions that were associated with the calming blend of essential oils. In time, after that initial processing had completed, I was more prepared to address the emotional healing that would take place with the use of the secondary, stronger smelling oil. Though the stressor hadn't necessarily been removed, my ability to process the emotions around the situation had progressed and been strengthened and healed through the support of implementing these essential oils.

This process of being drawn to specific oils and then finding an emotional growth and experiencing their healing properties has happened time and time again for me. I even find that oils that I am drawn to can greatly lose their appeal even just after a short period of implementing energy healing or meditation, because only a short amount was necessary to support the healing that needed to take place. I know that this is one simple technique that can be used to enhance intuition and even identify the emotional healing we are prepared to address.

I will explain this introductory and yet enlightening method to increase our personal awareness to our own body and spirit's intuition.

In order to identify the emotional needs we are ready to release, the book *Emotions and Essential Oils* is necessary. By this point, you may have collected some oils you have started implementing into your physical, emotional, and energy healing. Gather those and then find a quiet spot to relax. I've done this seated and even a couple times while relaxing in a bath.

Make sure that you have three designated spots to sort the essential oils; one for those you're drawn to, one for those you are repulsed by, and those that fit neither category. If you want, close your eyes or you can turn the lights off completely for the first portion of this technique. Do whatever you feel most comfortable with. Our vision greatly affects our other senses, so closing your eyes releases the expectations.

As you begin, pause for a moment to meditate or pray to connect yourself with the God of your understanding. Then, you will begin separating the oils. Without looking at the label of oil you pick up, open the bottle and smell it carefully. Often, you will find that some scents you will may quickly identify and others you will not recognize. As you smell the oil, determine if it is one you are drawn to, repelled by, or neutral about. Being drawn to a specific oil doesn't always mean that these are the oils with the 'prettiest' odors. It means that this is an essential oil that you feel a pull towards, an energy shift, or just desire to smell repeatedly.

Begin to recognize your body's intuitive abilities and powers. Notice how there is a noticeable difference in your physical, emotional, and spiritual response or reaction. Take time to do this with each essential oil. You will probably notice that most oils only take one or two inhales before you can categorize them.

Once you are done with this categorizing process, go through the oils you were drawn to and also the oils that you were repulsed by a couple more times to narrow it down even more. Put away the oils that were categorized as neutral. I would try to aim for narrowing it down to two or three oils if you have never done this process before. If you are more experienced with using essential oils, you may find yourself with a handful or so. This way you can narrow it down to those oils that you are truly ready for.

The essential oils that you were drawn to correlate with the emotional healing that your body, spirit, and energy are ready and prepared for. The oils that you are repulsed by are emotions that you bear or carry. These emotions may still need some time, additional work, or support before they are ready to be directly addressed. We are going to use both groups of oils at this time to promote healing.

Feel free to open your eyes or turn the lights back on now. Look at the essential oils you have identified. Begin with those oils that you are repulsed by. Look at the corresponding information within *Emotions and Essential Oils.* As you are reading about each oil, take time to briefly inhale or apply the oil. Because these are oils that do not smell appealing, if you choose to apply them, feel free to apply them to the bottom of the feet or a part of the body where the scent will not be cumbersome to you.

By beginning with these oils, you are aiding and augmenting the process of preparing for the emotional healing that the spirit, mind, and body need. Make sure to read through and take time experiencing and inhaling each oil you set aside in this group, whether it is one oil or several.

Now, turn to the group of essential oils that is appealing to you. Repeat this same process with these oils by reading about each in the *Emotions and Essential Oils* book while applying them and inhaling them. When inhaling these oils, because you are drawn to them, apply in correlating body areas or chakras. For example, if you are drawn to Geranium oil, which is an oil that encourages love and increases trust, you can apply it over the heart or heart chakra. It is an oil that helps to open the heart. Feel free to apply these oils to whatever part of the body you feel inspired to with caution used for those hot oils.

Take time with each oil. Allow tears to flow if, while reading, something penetrates and touches you. Pause with moments like these and just inhale the oil. Express gratitude for the tools to heal and the opportunity to learn from any corresponding emotions or experiences.

After experiencing and taking time with each oil, close with a prayer or meditation. Recognize the love that the Divine has for you, your potential, your path, and your purpose. Express gratitude for the gift to identify and be able to clear these emotions in a safe place.

This process can be repeated often if desired. As we experience new things each day that we allow to affect us, we can constantly be shifting the places where emotional healing is necessary and ready.

As you do this more frequently and become more familiar with your sense of intuition, you may begin to find that the process can be performed more quickly. You may find that you can simply ask your body or the Divine what oil you need, and you will find an answer come to mind. When you get to this point, feel free to test it. Test it by taking time to actually smell the oil, look up the corresponding information, and see how you resonate with it. The process will become more fine-tuned with time and experience. Make sure each time this is done to express gratitude for the tools, knowledge, and power to recognize the intuitive gifts and abilities your body, mind, and spirit has to address its own needs.

***

Note: We highly recommend using the book
***Emotions & Essential Oils*. It is a pivotal part of**
understanding the healing power of the essential

oils and will be helpful in doing the exercises we share in this book.

Healing Tools
&
Techniques

Methods of Essential Oil Application

Before using essential oils, it is important to educate yourself on the application of them and the variety of ways to do so. The essential oils that we work with are very pure and therapeutic grade. We would caution that you look at the label of any essential oil you might use to see if it is safe for ingestion or for topical use on the skin before using it in either way. The oils we use are in their purest form and very safe and effective.

We would even go as far as saying that the purest form of essential oils you can find will be the most effective in helping emotionally. The purer they are, the higher the frequency and effectiveness in doing what they are supposed to in order to support your body in its natural way of healing physically and emotionally. You will have far better results with the purest forms of essential oils. This is pertinent.

Topically

Direct application onto the skin is one of the easiest ways to use essential oils. It is highly effective since essential oils can easily pass through the lipid membranes of cell walls. They are able to penetrate cells and disperse throughout the body within seconds. Since one of the areas on the body with the largest pores is the feet, the bottom of the feet is a good place to apply oils directly. It is also because many nerve endings from the entire body are found there.

Before you start, remember to test a small area of the skin first. Apply one oil or blend at a time. When layering oils that are new to you, allow 2-3 minutes between each oil application to give the body a chance to respond before applying a second oil.

The longer that essential oils stay in contact with the skin, the more likely they are to be absorbed. Don't wash them off too soon.

Carrier oils are organic oils that are used to carry the oil to a greater surface area of the skin. When massaging, the carrier oil helps lubricate the skin, as well. These can easily be found at a local grocery or health foods store. Some suggested carrier oils are:

· Olive Oil
· Coconut Oil
· Sesame Oil
· Wheat Germ Oil

· Almond Oil
· Grapeseed (cold-pressed) Oil
· Jojoba Oil

When applying essential oils to children, always use a carrier oil. Lavender oil does not require dilution as long as it is not lavandin or genetically-engineered lavender. Add 15-30 drops of essential oil to one ounce of a quality carrier oil and mix well.

How to Dispense Essential Oils

Hold the bottle of oil 1 to 4 inches above the fingers or palm of the other hand. Tip the bottle over and wait for the oil to drip out. Then, massage the oil onto the desired area. Oil can also be dropped directly over the body in this way, such as the back or other parts of the body.

Some essential oils are thicker than others and require a gentle shake. Make sure to never touch the center of the drop dispenser -- let the oil drip from the edge freely. This ensures that the pure essential oil remaining in the bottle is not contaminated by the oils from your skin. Also make sure to not leave bottles open without a cap. They do evaporate.

Layering

Multiple oils can be applied, one at a time, using a technique called layering. For example, if marjoram is used on a sore muscle, it is massaged into the tissue until the area is dry. Then the next oil is applied - perhaps lemongrass, until the oil is absorbed. Then the third oil, possibly basil, until the oil is absorbed. This step can be continued with as many oils as necessary or desired.

Massage

Mix 3-4 drops of essential oil with ½ tsp. of a massage oil blend or carrier oil to create custom massage oil. Whenever you go get a massage, have the massage therapist add some essential oils to their massage oil or lotion and experience a massage like no other!

Diffusing/Aromatherapy

Diffusing essential oils is a perfect way to improve your home, work, or living environment. Diffusing can purify the air and neutralize mildew, cigarette smoke or other odors, as well as protect you and your family from viruses and bacteria. This is one of the most effective ways to support emotional healing with essential oils.

Inhalation/Aromatherapy Techniques

· Place 2 or more drops into the palm of one hand and rub your hands together. Cup hands together over the nose and mouth and inhale deeply.

· Place 2 or 3 drops of essential oil in a cool mist diffuser in a room in your home.

· Add several drops of an essential oil to a bowl of hot (not boiling) water. Inhale the vapors that rise from the bowl. A towel can be placed over the head and bowl to increase the intensity of the vapors.

· Apply a few drops of essential oil to a cotton ball, tissue, natural-fiber handkerchief, or clay necklace and inhale periodically.

· Apply 2 or more drops of oil anywhere on your upper body, such as chest, neck, sternum, under nose and ears or wrists. Breathe in the fragrance throughout the day.

Emotional Application Techniques

Emotions are processed in the 3 'brains' of the body: the mind, the heart, and the gut. When using essential oils for emotional purposes, you can also apply them directly to one, two, or all three of these areas as inclined.

For the mind, you can apply the essential oil to the top of the head, temples, base of the skull, or behind the ears.

For the heart, simply rub a drop right over your heart or sternum area.

For the gut, you can apply it to any area of the stomach from right under the ribcage to the top of the pubic crest.

Breathing

We've just covered essential oil use. Since we are using aromatherapy with the oils, we have already discussed how it affects the emotional part of the brain through smell. Let's now discuss breathing and how important that is in relaxing and healing, and the significance of breathing in through the nose, before we go to the healing techniques.

Controlled breathing not only keeps the mind and body functioning at their best, it can also lower blood pressure, promote feelings of calm and relaxation, and—if we play our lungs right— help us de-stress.

Two of the many reasons breathing is important are because it supplies our bodies and organs with the oxygen necessary for survival, and it rids our bodies of waste products. Oxygen is essential for our brain, glands, nerves, and internal organs. If the brain is deprived of oxygen, it can damage other organs and systems in our body. Lack of oxygen is a major cause of heart disease, strokes, and cancer.

I have noticed that when I am experiencing emotions of overwhelm, frustration, anxiety, and stress, my breathing becomes strained. I wasn't even aware of the physical response my body was expressing until a friend pointed this out to me. I would rest between breaths and then just take deep, exacerbated breaths. It wasn't an even, calm, breathing pattern. My breathing was directly correlating with the stressed emotions I was experiencing.

Breathing is absolutely vital to our physical health, but it also correlates closely with our emotions. Our body responds physically to our emotions whether we are aware of it or not, and our emotions are affected by our physical body in return.

When I became aware of my strained breathing, I paused and took a few moments to focus on relaxing it. I focused on my body's physical response and on each inhale and exhale so that they flowed continuously, rhythmically, and relaxed.

Once my breathing was under control, I realized that my emotions had settled significantly as well. My mind was calmer. I didn't feel as if I were emotionally drowning and 'gasping' for air. I had figuratively stood up in the water I felt I was drowning in, and was able to calmly recognize the solutions, direction, and peace that had been available to me the whole time.

Progressive Relaxation

The type of breathing technique to become familiar with using these tools, and with Aromatherapy, is called ***Progressive Relaxation.***

How it's done: To let go of tension from head to toe, close your eyes and focus on tensing and relaxing each muscle group for two to three seconds each. Start with the feet and toes, then move up to the knees, thighs, rear, chest, arms, hands, neck, jaw, and eyes—all while maintaining deep, slow breaths. Having trouble staying on track? Anxiety and panic specialist Dr. Patricia Farrell suggests we breathe in through the nose, hold for a count of five while the muscles tense, and then breathe out through the mouth on release.[7]

Healing Environment

The following tools will be very helpful in clearing yourself of non-beneficial energy and past experiences that may have carried pain with them. There are guidelines to using these tools to achieve maximum benefit. Make sure to give yourself plenty of time to use the tools. If you are teaching these techniques to others, either one on one or in a group setting, make sure to allow for plenty of time to relax and then process the tools so that there is a feeling of completeness in using the process. I want to stress how important it is that these exercises are performed in a quiet space away from noise and distractions, so that you can completely process what you need to. I also want to encourage you to let feelings flow and to allow tears to flow if they need to. It's important to feel the emotions that arise from doing these exercises; it is part of the releasing process. I would encourage you to do the exercises on yourself first so you can experience their healing power and practice them on people close to you until you feel comfortable performing them in a class with others.

Visualization is necessary to heal energetically, and to connect the mind with the body. Each of these exercises requires you to close your eyes for most of the duration in order for the process to feel complete.

It is recommended that you read through each exercise before actually performing it to familiarize yourself with it. You may feel more comfortable having someone read it for you and guiding you through it.

We have shared some of our own experiences with energy healing and have educated you about how essential oils can heal. We then guided you through the proper use of essential oils and breathing techniques. These are all pieces to the puzzle that encompass inner healing. Now it's time to fit it all together. As you go through each exercise, you will see the different layers of healing yourself, as you use each exercise to help heal emotions and experiences within you. Each exercise is designed to be simple and easy to use in the comfort of your own home. The reason we wrote this book was to literally bring healing to the world by empowering people to start taking healing into their own hands. These simple techniques are great beginners' tools in doing so. We acknowledge that more in depth healing can be accomplished through more intensive energy healing sessions, but also assure you that these tools provide a great start on the road to empowering you in your own healing. We have each experienced our own healing from these exercises and are excited to share these with the world.

Each exercise is described in a step by step process, so you can easily use them for yourself and those close to you. As you experience them, you will see subtle emotional changes within you, and possibly healing on a deeper level. Effects vary from person to person, in part based on how prepared you feel you are to heal and let go.

Diffusing

Since we have discussed how effective pure essential oils are through inhalation and getting to the limbic system "the emotional part of the brain" we highly suggest diffusing the oils during each exercise to help support and create a wonderful healing environment that we know can potentially accelerate the healing process. While the oils are diffusing, it creates a calmness in the body and in the emotions. I often diffuse the oils at night while I sleep and it's amazing how calm and refreshed I feel in the morning as I have essentially given myself some Aromatherapy while sleeping. Diffusing the oils is a very powerful healing tool and I use them often during sessions with clients in order to support their own healing and create the most beneficial healing environment. I will often choose a particular oil because of its beneficial emotional properties that pertain to what my client may be experiencing. For example, Rosemary is the oil of transition so I will diffuse it in my office while I'm working with a client who may be going through a huge transition in their life. I cannot live without my diffuser. It is definitely a must in my practice and in my home!

Healing Tool #1

Releasing Identified Burdens

This tool provides a way that we can release and heal those stressors, weights, and patterns that are limiting our progress. There have been times when I feel stuck or am struggling to move forward. I may be moving forward, but it feels strained as if I am trudging through thick deep mud up to my knees or sometimes even up to my chest, often affecting my breathing and endurance. I can even tell exactly what it is sometimes that's stopping me from running free.

For example, I was raised in a very loving home, but it lacked structure when it came to routines and cleanliness. My mother was raised in a similar home herself and the pattern may reach even further back. As a result, this 'generational pattern' is something I was aware of, but didn't know how to change. It weighed me down. Housekeeping was a huge drudge more than it should be because I didn't have routines in place, didn't have habits of any sort for cleaning or scheduling, and didn't have the natural know-how. It was a strained effort constantly.

This is a "chain" that limited me. My spirit functions naturally and thrives with order and structure. The body and mortal being took on this 'chain' as a limiting weight because of the family patterns I experienced, but I didn't need to carry it throughout my life. This tool allows you to release these chains.

Other examples of limiting chains could be self-loathing, grudges, stresses, sorrow, or sadness from a specific experience, lingering guilt from issues that have already been properly resolved, heartache, or negative cycles or habits that are stressful or limiting. There may even be other issues or circumstances that you have been in or are in that have left a 'chain'. This tool is to aid in releasing these.

Through the gift of Divine love and light, we do not need to suffer through these. We do not need to be limited or weighed down. Divine love wants us to succeed and experience abundance in every positive way. Divine love wants to lighten our load so that we can.

Dissolving Chains

Just to reiterate, there are times in our life where we can see what is blocking our progression or weighing us down, but we aren't fully sure of the tools to release it and move past it. These blocks may include things like stressors in our life, generational patterns we've inherited, or even just sorrows or hardness we are carrying around in our heart. We know what the issue at hand is, and we don't want to hold on to it any longer, but don't know what to do to rid ourselves of the burden. These burdens hold us down and weigh on us like chains. This is an inspired tool to help remove those weights halting our growth, progression, peace, and happiness.

There are several oils that you can implement as we complete this exercise.

Essential Oils to choose from for this healing tool:

White Fir- helps to release patterns that have been passed on through the family line generationally and breaks toxic cycles

Comforting Blend- this oil helps in consoling the soul and to help it heal from loss and the effects of grief, helps in releasing trauma from the past

Geranium- helps in creating trust in ourselves and in others and the ability to love again and allowing the heart to heal

Calming Blend- this oil contains a blend that is helpful in forgiving the self and others and releasing grudges of the past and releasing control

Thyme- helpful in dissolving pain and anger and softening the bitter heart in order to forgive

Basil- helpful in bringing courage and strength to the overwhelmed heart in order to forge ahead through difficulties

Wintergreen- this oil helps in releasing the illusion of wanting to control and allowing oneself to connect to their Creator and know that they are not alone

Lemongrass- helpful in clearing and cleansing the energy that feels heavy around us and assists in dissipating darkness that keeps us from gaining clarity

For after this exercise:

Encouraging blend- this oil motivates the soul to want to create and to bring clarity of purpose to mind body and soul and the energy to carry it out

Uplifting blend- this oil lightens the load of heaviness in the soul and creates an uplifting mood and the ability to let go of the things that weigh us down.

To purchase essential oils please go to:
www.aromaheal.org

Exercise

Diffuse any oil of your choosing to accelerate the healing taking place emotionally through the limbic system as you inhale the oils that are diffused. This can also be used instead of applying the oil topically in case you have an aversion to any oils.

Pick the essential oil that you are drawn to most. Apply one drop in your hand and rub your hands together in a circular motion. Then, take one deep breath and inhale the healing essential oil. Rub your hand on your heart to apply some essential oil to it and then once again cup your hands and inhale again. This may be done with several oils if you feel prompted or inspired.

To begin this exercise now, find a comfortable and quiet sitting position. Sit with your eyes closed for a moment and set your intention for this exercise. This can be done by saying out loud, or in your mind something like, "My intention is to find healing as I complete this exercise."

Now, softly close your eyes. Take a deep breath. Ponder the burdens you are carrying that you are ready to release. These may be burdens of sorrow, stress, an argument, hard words heard or spoken, thoughts limiting you, patterns passed on from family, heartaches, feelings of worthlessness or inadequacy, or whatever it may be limiting you or weighing you down. (Pause)

Imagine each of those burdens as chains weighing you down and keeping you from moving forward and upward. These chains are wrapped around your heart, arms, legs, mind, and parts of your body—each one weighing you down. Limiting you. Label each chain. Identify it. Know exactly what it is and how it is limiting you. (Pause)

Then, recognize and picture the great healing light of the Divine. This healing light is a light of healing love. Love that encompasses all that we are and all that we can become. This is an unconditional and eternal love that extends beyond our own comprehension. This love is powerful. Feel as it begins to help loosen the chains that bind you.

Imagine this light of love stretching forth towards you. As you see it, begin to unravel the chains that have been binding you down. One by one, hand them over to this healing light. With each chain, as you hand it over, watch it disintegrate right before your eyes. That once binding chain is now completely dissolved and no longer exists. Do this with each chain taking time to identify what it is you are handing over to the Divine light of love and watching your divine release you from that bind, and dissolve the chain.

When each chain is completely removed from you and dissolved in the light of divine love, imagine this divine light of love gathering into a beautiful ball. Take this ball and accept it into your heart. Once there, look and see how it doesn't just stay isolated in your heart, but it begins to spread throughout your entire body. Reaching all the way down to your toes, to your fingertips, and the top of your head. This divine light begins to extend even beyond that and stretches upward once again toward the heavens and connects you to the Divine.

Now, see yourself filled with this powerful healing light, standing and stretching tall, and standing firm in your renewed strength. No longer held down by the chains that burdened you and limited you. You are free to move forward and complete your purpose and mission with love, light, joy, peace, trust, and comfort.

Take your hand and touch it to your heart accepting this Divine love and gift. Say out loud, "I release what has limited me and now fully accept the support of Divine love."

Inhale the scent from your hand three more times. Take this moment, as you're inhaling, to savor the beautiful gift you've received.

When you are ready, you may open your eyes.

Apply Encouraging Blend or Uplifting Blend to your feet after this exercise.

Healing Tool #2

Unconditional Love

One of the most beautiful spiritual gifts or tools is that of unconditional love. This is one of the most powerful healing tools to both give and receive. It is the ability to love and receive love without expectations, attachments, or assumptions. When we can feel and give love free of all expected outcomes, responses, and reactions, good or negative, we are able to truly serve, heal and touch others in a divine way. Our heart's ability to love, comfort, console, and heal is powerful.

Heart stones

There are experiences we have throughout our life that can put a block around our heart. These experiences over time can build up a wall. If there is a specifically traumatic experience, this wall can be built quickly in almost its entirety. This blocks us from both giving and receiving of that powerful love. Sometimes it is blocked towards specific individuals and other times it is even blocking love inward that we can receive or give ourselves. At times we can identify the experiences that limit our ability to give and receive love fully, but at other times they may be subtle events that we subconsciously have pushed down.

This tool is a beautiful and simple technique that can be used to have this wall around the heart taken away and refueled with love and light. This allows us to be able to feel love for and from others with a greater capacity. It allows us to serve as a divine instrument of love in the lives of those around us more constructively and fully.

Essential oils that are recommended to be utilized with this tool:

Renewing Blend- this oil contains of blend of oils that promote forgiveness and a letting go of old wounds from the past that have festered the soul. It is freeing and creates a sense of feeling grounded
Comforting Blend- this oil helps in consoling the soul and to help it heal from loss and the effects of grief, helps in releasing trauma from the past
Geranium- helps in creating trust in ourselves and in others and the ability to love again and allowing the heart to heal
Calming Blend- this oil contains a blend that is helpful in forgiving the self and others and releasing grudges of the past and letting go of control

Thyme- helpful in dissolving pain and anger and softening the bitter heart in order to forgive

Rose- this oil brings healing to the wounded heart and helps it to become open to giving and receiving love in all aspects

Cedarwood- this oils helps a person to feel surrounded and supported by others and to open the heart to connecting with others

Bergamot- this oils helps one gain confidence in self and acceptance of the body and strength within

Frankincense- this oil helps a person to be honest with themselves and others, to live in integrity and connect with God and open their heart to His messages

For after this exercise:

Encouraging blend- this oil motivates the soul to want to create and to bring clarity of purpose to mind body and soul and the energy to carry it out

Uplifting blend- this oil lightens the load of heaviness in the soul and creates an uplifting mood and the ability to let go of the things that weigh us down.

To purchase essential oils please go to
www.aromaheal.org

Exercise

It might be beneficial to diffuse an oil of your choosing to accelerate the healing process as you inhale the oil being diffused. This is calming to the limbic system.

As we begin this exercise, choose which oil most resonates with you and find a comfortable position either seated or lying on your back. Take one drop of the essential oil you chose and with your right hand, rub the drop of essential oil over your heart. Close your eyes. Then, hold your hand in place over your heart and take three deep cleansing breaths in and out. Feel your heart beating under your hand. Recognize the power that it holds, that you carry within yourself.

With your eyes still closed, rest your hands down to your side.

Picture yourself in a large beautiful white space. It is radiating light, energy, and healing from all sides of you. Allow this light to comfort, wrap, and envelop you in its warmth and love. (Pause)

Now, in front of you is a bright light of healing divine love. It is radiating, beautiful and here to aid you specifically. This divine light of love desires to serve you and remove these walls burdening you and limiting your ability to give and receive of love fully and unconditionally. From this beautiful light extends a gentle, loving hand. Invite and welcome it to reach into your heart space so that it can remove each stone that has been built up around your heart. One at a time, watch this divine hand of love and light reach in and lovingly remove the stone wall from around your heart. You may recognize exactly what experience or person the stones relate to, or you may not. Allow divine love to remove it regardless so that greater healing can be received.

One at a time, watch as the stone literally crumbles in the hand of this divine love and dissolves into a beautiful purple and silver flame of light before disappearing.

Allow this hand, reaching from pure, divine love, to continue removing the heart stones until you feel complete. Repeat the beautiful process with each stone that is removed, identifying it if you are able, and then watching it be beautifully destroyed through the power of divine love.

When the stones are removed, watch as this divine hand of love and light gathers in all the healing light and love it has emanated from into a beautiful, brightly, glowing ball. Allow this hand to then fill your heart space with this beautiful ball of healing light. Allow it to softly, and lovingly place this light into your heart space with great care, filling the void where the stones once were.

Allow this hand of divine love to now rest on your heart as you take three deep breaths. Place your hand on top of the divine hand of love and light over your heart, thanking it for the beautiful healing it has allowed you to receive today. Take three more breaths with your hand there as you thank it and express your gratitude.

With your eyes still closed and your hand still resting on your heart, repeat out loud or in your mind the following:

I love.
I am love.
I am loved.
I am loved by the divine.
I am divine.
I am healed.

Take two more deep breaths. Rest your hand down by your side once again. When you are ready, you may open your eyes.

Apply Encouraging Blend or Uplifting Blend to the bottom of your feet after this exercise.

True Healing

"By choosing your thoughts, and by selecting which emotions you release and which you will reinforce, you determine the quality of your Light. You determine the effect you will have on others, and the nature of the experience of your life."
-Gary Zukav

True healing contains four crucial parts on your end for permanent healing to take place: accountability, forgiveness, gratitude and love.

We as humans tend to be pain avoiders. We think we aren't supposed to experience pain for some reason so we work to really avoid it, especially when it involves a loss in our lives. We are taught how to acquire things but not how to lose things. When we lose things we shut down and try to avoid. Quite honestly though, the quickest way to get through pain is to literally walk through it, feel it, and move forward.

Before I, Christi, became The Healing Coach, I worked for a non-profit organization where I facilitated many clients experiencing sudden trauma, tragedy and loss. Very often I saw them go numb to avoid the pain or do things to numb themselves. This is a much more painful path to choose.

I want you to imagine getting a big ugly gash in your leg and it starts to bleed. Instead of sitting down and taking care of it, cleaning it out and then bandaging it so it can heal, you decide to put Novocain on it to numb it so that you don't feel the pain. Weeks go by and you have numbed it over and over and over until one day it has become infected with gangrene and you end up in the hospital with a huge horrible infection that may even need to be amputated. Now there is more work to be done in order to heal it and it has caused even more harm and damage to your body. This is how pain can destroy us when we don't stop and deal with it. If we continue to numb ourselves from it and push it down, it will show up in a bigger way 10 times worse later on with bigger wounds to heal that may cause us even more damage emotionally.

When I worked for the non-profit organization years ago, I had a father come in who had lost a child tragically to a drunk driver crash who hit them head on and soon after wanted to volunteer full time. Day after day he helped our organization tremendously and I noticed he had a tendency to be a workaholic. I grew up with one so I knew the signs well. I tried several times to talk to him about the death of his child and encouraged him to go to support group but he avoided all of it. I was concerned that one day it would all come crashing down around him if he didn't deal with the deep pain from this horrific tragedy. Nearly a year later, after avoiding it for so long, he had a nervous breakdown and his life has never been the same since. It was so much more painful for him because his mechanism was to avoid. My heart broke for him.

We must not be avoiders of pain.

The extreme opposite of that is just as detrimental. Imagine that same wound throbbing and causing unbearable pain. Instead of looking to heal it, you keep screaming about how painful it is and you desire everyone to look at it because it hurts you so much. Day in and day out, you do nothing to heal. You continue to talk about how painful it is and show everyone how gory and horrible the wound is without ever trying to fix it. When you focus completely on your pain, you use all your energy and have nothing left to focus on anything else in your life. This can be very damaging not only to you, but to the people around you. Taking the time to address it, to care for it, and then heal it allows you to give energy to the healing process and frees up space to focus on other aspects of your life as well. Don't allow the pain from past experiences to rule your life today or in your future. Seek to find the healing you deserve. Otherwise you become a prisoner to your pain and the pain others have caused you, which in turn, gives away your power to heal.

Clearing away the darkness and heaviness of low vibration emotions and experiences we can't seem to let go of makes me think of literally lifting the fog so we can see the sunshine. It's a process of no longer living in denial of all that needs to be acknowledged. Think of yourself walking into a fog where you can't see the next step in front of you. As you release the darkness that fogs your ideas, thoughts, and mind, things become more clear. You gain clarity and you are able to discern better and distinguish more clearly. I pondered this thought one day "The glory of God is in intelligence." It really hit me as I understood that with more knowledge comes more light and as you use it for the good, your knowledge increases. When knowledge increases, the light increases and you gain more understanding as opposed to "staying in the dark" about things.

As darkness sets into a room, it engulfs the light, you have no direction because you can't even see what is in front of you. When you walk into a completely dark room, there is no direction or even a glimmer of where to walk next. Light gives us direction out of the dark. As you increase the light, you even become "LIGHTER" yourself. I know that after people have done sessions with me, they experience a "lightness" about them because they let go of the energy that was literally "weighing" them down. Their countenance even changes and there is more brightness in their eyes and complexion. Taking away the fog of darkness truly increases enlightenment and decreases heaviness. Adding the oils to the experience of healing and clearing the darkness can be pivotal in increasing the light as well.

Accountability

"More people would learn from their mistakes if they weren't so busy denying them"
-Harold J. Smith

Years ago, I was reading all the right books and saying affirmations and trying to convince myself that I really was rich when I wasn't or that I was very successful when I didn't feel successful inside. I was doing all the right things but I hadn't done the inner work to believe for myself that I deserved all that I was wanting in my life.

The most powerful results I have ever experienced are when I finally come to the place of acknowledgement about an issue I have tried to stay in denial of. When this happens, I can finally resolve it and find healing in it to then apply the self-development tools that can make me successful in creating all that I want in life. I keep learning the same lessons until it finally becomes too painful to ever want to experience it again. So I face it head on, and do the healing work to clear it to bring the darkness to the forefront that I haven't wanted to face, in order to embrace the light. When we literally shed light on a topic that has brought us so much pain and darkness, we are revealing the truth behind what it has done in stumping our growth and progress, and allowing it to no longer have power in our lives.

As we clear away the weeds that have choked our garden of thoughts and clear the ground, we make space for newer seeds to be planted that produce more fruitful outcomes in our life. When I work with my clients, I explain how when we get to the root of the belief that began long before they ever came into a session with me, then we can clear all the weeds that continue to choke all the positivity we are trying to create in our lives. We can plant millions of positive thoughts and tell ourselves hundreds of affirmations, but until we clear out the weeds that have grown around this, the garden won't be clear for us to see all the plants and the flowers that have been growing. Weeds can take over and choke the very thing we worked so hard to create because we didn't get rid of what was choking it in the first place.

We don't seem to want to acknowledge our own accountability when in truth, it is the most freeing feeling to finally acknowledge the truth about ourselves and our pain. That is when the most growth and progress happens!

Taking accountability for the pain we have caused others can be a way to face the pain rather than avoid it. It's interesting how so many find it difficult to take accountability for their actions and choices. Pride sets in and they don't want to admit any wrong doing on their end, yet this is how we stay prisoners to pain. Accountability can be one of the most freeing things you can do for yourself. Admit your weaknesses and move forward. Take accountability for the pain you have also caused yourself. Live in shame no more. Shame only holds you in a place to avoid the healing you so deserve. Let go of shame and free yourself!

The more you acknowledge, the more you can clear out and let go of. I see so much pain in the world daily as I work with others to help them release it. So much pain is caused by not taking accountability. When you don't take accountability, the same cycles of pain continue over and over and are even passed on generationally, affecting our children and grandchildren and so on because we don't let go and learn to do anything different than what we have always done. So much pain can be released if we would just take accountability for our own actions. Taking accountability really is about refusing to lie to ourselves anymore about why we really do things or how we really treat people. Accountability means being honest about ourselves and our actions. It is accepting that we aren't perfect.

Forgiveness

"Some of us think holding on makes us strong, but sometimes it is letting go."
- Herman Hesse

Forgiveness is such a key to moving forward. Healing can't take place without forgiveness being present. Honestly, in all the work I've done with hundreds of clients, I have realized that the number one area of forgiveness that needs to take place is forgiveness of self. It is hands down the most powerful place to begin the healing process and to gain the most results. It is only in forgiveness of self first, that fully loving oneself can begin.

People get confused about forgiveness and what it actually is. Sometimes we have the impression that we are letting someone "get away with it" when we forgive the wrong-doing. Forgiveness does not justify the wrong act, nor does it ignore the other person's responsibility. People can be forgiven without excusing their harmful act of behavior.

"True forgiveness has very little to do with the other person, it has to do with you- the forgiver. Forgiveness is a way to let go of negative emotions, resentment, anger and even thoughts of revenge. Until you forgive, the act that hurt you in the first place will continue to be a part of your life. Forgiveness loosens the 'grip' that the original pain has on you so that you can refocus on the positive aspects of your life. At its best, forgiveness will lead you to empathy, understanding and compassion for the person who harmed you. Forgiveness will bring you peace about a person or situation so that you can go on with your life."[8]

According to Dr. Katherine Piderman of the Mayo Clinic[9], the price you pay for not forgiving can be very very high. If you're unforgiving you may pay the price repeatedly by bringing anger and bitterness into every relationship and new experience. Your life may become so wrapped up in the wrong that you can't enjoy the present. You may become depressed or anxious. You may feel that your life lacks meaning or purpose, or that you're at odds with your spiritual beliefs. You may lose valuable and enriching connectedness with others.

I liken forgiving and letting go of anger to ridding yourself of venom from a snake. If a poisonous snake bit you, would you chase after it to kill it for what it did to you while the poison is running through your veins and affecting you, or would you sit down immediately to get the venom out of you before it killed you? Anger, bitterness and unforgiveness can be the venom that eats away at us, and our energy, and destroys us, and our relationships.

Gratitude

Having a gratitude attitude has been linked to an increase in better health. Some of the benefits are less anxiety and depression, more sound sleep, higher long-term satisfaction with life and behaving kinder toward others, including your significant other. It has also been found that people who feel more grateful are less likely to become aggressive when provoked. Gratitude is an important part of healing. Look to be grateful for the lessons that life has taught you. Show gratitude for the experiences gained from them and even the people involved, and recognize what you have learned from them. When you do these things, rather than look at the lack or the deprivation the experience has brought you, you are in a better place to move forward.

Why do you think gratitude is key to healing?

"We must begin by learning what it means to have enough....to feel gratitude for having been born on a planet so rich in Nature and gratitude for the water that makes our life possible. If you open your eyes you will see that the world is full of so much that deserves our gratitude. When you have become the embodiment of gratitude, think about how pure the water that fills your body will be. When this happens you, yourself will be a beautiful shining crystal of light." -Masaro Emoto

In the book, *The Hidden Messages In Water*, Dr. Masara Emoto researched water extensively and found some remarkable results when he studied the effects of water from music and even the words that are spoken. He realized how much the words we use have a vibration and an affect on our bodies and ourselves. Here were his profound findings:

All the classical music that we exposed the water to resulted in well-formed crystals with distinct characteristics. In contrast, the water exposed to violent heavy metal music resulted in fragmented and malformed crystals at best.

But our experimenting didn't stop there. We next thought about what would happen if we wrote words or phrases like "Thank you" and "Fool" on pieces of paper and wrapped that paper around the bottles of water with the words facing in. It didn't seem logical for water to "read" the writing, understand the meaning, and change its form accordingly.

But I knew from the experiment with music that strange things could happen.

The results of the experiments didn't disappoint us. Water exposed to "Thank you" formed beautiful hexagonal crystals but water exposed to the word "Fool" produced crystals similar to the water exposed to heavy-metal music, malformed and fragmented.

I particularly remember one photograph. It was the most beautiful and delicate crystal that I had so far seen – formed by being exposed to the words "love and gratitude." It was as if the water had rejoiced and celebrated by creating a flower in bloom. It was so beautiful that I can say that it actually changed my life from that moment on.

Here is that photograph:

LOVE AND GRATITUDE

Used by permission by Office Masaru Emoto LLC

We all know that words have an enormous influence on the way we think and feel and that things generally go more smoothly when positive words are used. However, up until now, we have never been able to physically see the effect of words.

Words are very likely to have an enormous impact on the water that composes as much as seventy percent of our body, and this impact will in no small way affect our bodies.

If you fill your heart with love and gratitude, you will find yourself surrounded by so much that you can love and feel grateful for; you can get closer to enjoying the life of health and happiness. But what if you emit signals of hate, dissatisfaction, and sadness? Then you will probably find yourself in a situation that makes you hateful, dissatisfied, and sad.

The life you live and the world you live in are up to you.[10]

Gratitude can expand your heart to levels you never felt before, because a grateful heart helps you see into a world of learning and growth for life lessons that you came here to learn. It changes perspective and releases anger and bitterness.

Love

"Unconditional Love is obtained through the wholeness of your heart.
Self-Acceptance is received through the wholeness within you.
Freedom is acquired through the wholeness of your Being."
-Carolyn Greenleaf

Love truly is the most powerful force in the universe. I know it sounds cliché to say that love is what heals but truly it is love that heals us. We can't give what we don't have, so if we don't have love for ourselves, we don't have it to give to others.

In the remarkable research we just identified earlier with Dr. Emoto, he pointed out that the word Love created intricate icicles within water. Love has a high vibration energy to it just when the word itself is spoken. Love is what opens our hearts to new possibilities and what enters the space we emptied from non-beneficial energy when we do energy work. We are pulling out the weed that keeps choking our garden and putting in its place, something more positive and enriching. Love is the power to heal within yourself and gives you the strength and courage to move forward.

Love is and always has been the power and creative force of the universe. Creation does not exist without love. It is the very essence of love that brings creation into existence at all. Love is the actual force of the creation process and the power behind it. It is what brings the creation process into existence at all and is expansive and infinite. Since love is infinite in its expansion, it is always seeking to increase itself continually. Love is at the core of our own existence. It is the very seed from which light comes from and the light force in the universe.

Love does not see imperfections or look for what is wrong. From deep within the soul, at the core of who we are and within our truest selves, we see love as having no conditions, no expectations, no restrictions and no attachments; it only sees the truth of who we are, which is love actualized. Love does not recognize the false beliefs we tell ourselves, because unconditional love is all-encompassing and completely and fully accepting. It is the warm gentle blanket that embraces us from our Creator, loving us for who we are on all layers and all levels with absolutely no exceptions. We came from love and so it is love that we are constantly seeking because it is the core of what brought us into existence in the first place and love is the place from which we came. In the end, we naturally seek it because it is the very core of who we are.

I've seen ego represented as an acronym for **E**dging **G**od **O**ut. Because the ego cannot see beyond pain and fear from the past, it puts restrictions and conditions on its idea of love. Since the ego portrays God as a punishing or rewarding God, it identifies love the same way and with conditions upon it as well. The ego lives in lack and depletion while love lives in expansion and infinite possibilities. Love is nothing that is actualized by the ego. Since the ego can only identify with false experience and sometimes exaggerated perceptions, it cannot understand the concept of actual love. Because of this, the ego carries all of the pain and heartaches of past relationships into its new ones, judging it from those past experiences and relationships and therefore often dooming it. This is why we may continue to repeat patterns of attracting the same kinds of relationships that lack the love we seek. We judge our new relationships with the patterns we have seen in the past and don't let go of it.

Love truly is the most powerful healing tool any of us possess, because it is the highest vibration and frequency and contains the most pristine energy that exists in the universe. When the high vibration of love is present, it can transform anything of a non beneficial energy or nature because no creation made through the negative aspects that exist in the ego can exist in the energy of love's high vibration. Just as light and dark cannot exist in the same space so it is the same with the aspect of the ego and love. Love naturally exists to continue to create, whereas the ego many times stunts the growth within. Love is the transformational key within us and all that exists. Nothing has the power to transform as love does. It is so transformational that it can take something negative within us and turn it into something positive and beneficial, creating a more healing energy. Any and all effects from the ego's system having to do with physical being, emotional and mental states that have caused us problems can be transformed through the high vibration of love and create powerful healing and positive effects within the body and soul.

In her book *Re-Entering Eden- Reclaiming Our Wholeness and Divine Truth*, author Carolyn M. Greenleaf describes perfectly the power of love in the following excerpt:

"Love is the Light inside the seed that exists within everything. Even if it appears negative, someone who was not in recognition of his or her truth created it, and through the Soul, which exists within everyone, it automatically plants that seed even in the darker of creations. When we choose to water that seed of love, give it sunshine, and tend to it, we will see it change. It is the same as you nurturing and increasing your own Light vibration through the tending of love. The love we feel for ourselves also transmutes the negative energy within our cells and restores our body to its healthy state. Just as Snow White eats the poisoned apple and falls asleep, she awakens restored through the power of love.

"The wounds we suffer from today stem from two things, lack of love and acceptance. All we've ever wanted was to be seen as beautiful, brilliant, valuable, and precious children. There is no blame to be placed on anyone. Our parents or others in our life reacted to us the only way they knew how. They too were suffering from the lack of love and acceptance. We should not blame ourselves either, we came here through the same veil of forgetfulness that all humans do. Here, we start fresh, with the option of discovering our truth and expanding our light and wisdom by partaking of the Tree of Life, or walking with humanity through its pains and trials of the past by choosing to receive the fruit from the Tree of Knowledge of Good and Evil. Our Soul knows our Spirit's objective for this reality and planned what was needed to experience this, including the people and circumstances that it had to include. It was our journey through the shadows of this world that pushed us to reach higher than we thought we could. Our search for something better pushed us to create new paths. Our drive to survive the next attack grew our strength and determination from the inside out. Through our heart wrenching experience, we learned compassion and held out hope for a stranger in need.

"Now we can return to the Light within ourselves and choose again. Older and wiser and battle scarred, tattered and torn, we can always return to Eden. We have the ability to go back to discover and remember who we really are. Our true essence. We can return to the Light within and grow it bigger and brighter than the stars and the moon above. We have the ability to give to ourselves what we couldn't receive from this world. It is time for us to discover our hidden treasures and the truth that lies within."[11]

Love is the answer in creating the Light within. It is the strongest power and force on earth to do so. Love is always the answer when asked the question of how to return to our true selves, our essence. It is the beautiful, exquisite healing power within love that truly transforms all.

A Word On Generational Healing

We are going to touch a little on generational healing in this book and expand more on it in our third book. Generational healing can be so helpful for many. Just as things are passed onto us generationally through our DNA, so are things passed onto us energetically through our ancestors. If one person has the belief that spiders are scary and another person thinks no such thing, where is the difference and where did it come from? Their belief system. Our belief system (again, our B.S.) is what we take into any given situation in our life. It shapes our attitudes and the morals we live by. We pass onto our children many of our beliefs. Even beliefs in racism and discrimination can be passed on generationally. We get the belief from our parents, who got it from their parents, who got it from their parents and on and on. Our beliefs can keep us stuck generationally as well, and keep us in bondage from moving and progressing forward until we let go of our false beliefs.

Our belief system is filtered from our experiences, so we judge life and people and situations through the filter that formed from all of our life experiences. For instance, say I had a really bad experience in life with being betrayed over and over through friendships so I learned to not trust people and didn't make many friends. I carried this belief with me throughout life and when I became a mother, I put my belief system on my children and they kept to themselves. Because of my belief, I sheltered them and they in turn did not make many friends and when they did and were hurt in that relationship, I would say to them, "See, it never pays to have friends because they always betray you." I then reinforced it for my children who chose not to trust either and then they carried that same belief on to their children.

The same pertains to addictions and habits. These can create cycles and patterns within us that can be destructive and detrimental to us and our families. They continue to be passed on until they are destroyed or released. Going back to energy being stuck as we referred to in the beginning of this book, our ancestors had experiences as well where they didn't process emotions that were stuck within them and were never released. It affected them physically so as they had children, those were passed on as well. Something physical can even manifest in their children from those stuck emotions being passed on generationally. These all need to be released back to, and starting with, the person it was created with in the first place. As it is released generationally on an energetic level, then it releases it for all affected and touched by it. It is even more freeing to let go of things passed onto us generationally that never really belonged to us in the first place.

Thus, when we release things for ourselves, it is good to also include releasing things generationally as well to cover all bases and make the healing complete.

Healing Tool #3

Ho' Oponopono

When I was first introduced to this tool years ago, I was taken back by its simplicity. I wondered how something so simple could truly be so healing? Yet it simply is a miraculous and powerful tool. Through years of working with energy healing, I now realize how the power of speaking things out loud can be so strengthening to a soul. Using our voice can be such a tool in healing ourselves for as we speak, we create. Words have such power to them, in *The Hidden Messages of Water*, we learn that words have a vibration to them, and the words we speak to ourselves and others impact us even at our cellular level. Think about this though, if you have a negative thought about someone and then you speak it to them, who is the one with most harm done? You or them? You. Because it first was a thought created in your mind and then you spoke it, the negative thought, and the energy with it, went through you twice while they only received it once. In addition, since you are the one who created the negative thought, you have more power and feeling associated with it. They can choose to reject it and create a place where the negative thought never has any power over them from the beginning.

Ho'Oponopono[12] is an ancient Hawaiian practice of reconciliation and forgiveness. Similar forgiveness practices were performed on islands throughout the South Pacific, including Samoa, Tahiti and New Zealand.

These are the simple phrases to Ho'Oponopono which include four simple steps. The practice of speaking them out loud is important though nobody has to be physically present as you speak it and this is a very effective tool in healing and creating more peace in the heart. It can be useful in any aspect of your life whether it is a relationship, or an area that needs healing such as having anger issues or health issues or any area where you feel you may have contributed to the pain being caused in it.

1. **I'm sorry (Accountability)**
2. **Please Forgive Me (Forgiveness)**
3. **Thank You (Gratitude)**
4. **I Love You (Love)**

The technique we are sharing in this book with Ho'Oponopono takes it a step further than what is usually done with this process and brings more meaning and deeper healing to it as it is expounded upon here. Let me explain to you why. Imagine someone standing in front of you and needing to apologize to you. Which one would feel more sincere and powerful and healing to you? For them to just say "I'm sorry" or "I'm sorry for not acknowledging how I hurt your feelings and being so disrespectful to you. I should have chosen better. Please forgive me and let's work this out."? Which one feels more sincere and heartfelt? The second one is much more sincere because it is acknowledging our actions and accountability. Acknowledgment and accountability are crucial in releasing. Instead of avoiding our accountability we need to own it in order to free ourselves from it. Acknowledgement is such a powerful thing. We ALWAYS have a part in others offending or hurting us because we are the ones who choose to let it offend us.

Acknowledgement of our part in this helps us to let go of the chains that hold us back and it gives us humility that is helpful in letting go of the pride and un-forgiveness we hold onto.

Oils suggested for this exercise are:

Thyme- helpful in dissolving pain and anger and softening the bitter heart in order to forgive

Calming Blend- this oil contains a blend that is helpful in forgiving the self and others and releasing grudges of the past and letting go of control

Comforting Blend- this oil helps in consoling the soul and to help it heal from loss and the effects of grief, helps in releasing trauma from the past

Geranium- helps in creating trust in ourselves and in others and the ability to love again and allowing the heart to heal

Peppermint- helps to uplift the heavy heart and bring energy to the soul. It lightens those who feel weary and creates joy and a positive outlook

For after this exercise:

Encouraging blend- this oil motivates the soul to want to create and to bring clarity of purpose to mind body and soul and the energy to carry it out

Uplifting blend- this oil lightens the load of heaviness in the soul and creates an uplifting mood and the ability to let go of the things that weigh us down.

To purchase essential oils please go to

www.aromaheal.org

Exercise

Set your intention before you begin this healing tool. For example, "My intention is to find healing in my relationship with my mother" or "My intention is to help my body to heal as I let go and release forgiveness for ways in which I have harmed it or criticized it"

Apply an oil of your choosing to your heart area. Diffuse any oil of your choosing to accelerate the healing taking place emotionally through the limbic system as you inhale the oils that are diffused. This can also be used instead of applying the oil topically in case you have an aversion to any oils.

The process is to use each of the 4 phrases but in a more expressive and elaborative way.

Decide what or whom you are wanting to use the process on to find healing.

Elaborate with each phrase and work through each area that you need to.

Here are some examples:

If it's an issue with your health, it could work like this:

You can literally apologize to your body and address your body:

I'm sorry that I haven't given you the care you deserve by being more in tuned to you and your needs of exercise and nourishment and listening to what you were trying to tell me.

Please forgive me for not being more in tuned to you and acting upon it. Feel the forgiveness wash over you.

(After saying the "please forgive me" part, wait just a moment to feel the release of it and then proceed to the "Thank you" part)

Thank you for loving me and supporting me and helping me to do what I need to every day. Thank your body for all it does for you. Thank your cells. Thank yourself for being the best you can be. Thank God. Thank the Universe. Thank whatever it was that just forgave you. Just keep saying THANK YOU.

I love you and I am committing to loving you more by nourishing you properly. Say I LOVE YOU. Say it to your body, say it to God. Say I LOVE YOU to the air you breathe, to the house that shelters you. Say I LOVE YOU to your challenges. Say it over and over. Mean it. Feel it. There is nothing as powerful as Love.

This tool can also be used in situations where others have hurt us. We can still take ownership of any of our actions that may have contributed to any aspect of the situation.

For instance, I had a client who had a lot of anger and resentment towards her brother. He had made many poor choices that had affected her life and the lives of many, and he was still continuing to make these choices. She realized that there was a place within her that needed to heal from this. As I worked with her, I helped her to understand that sometimes we will never understand the pain that brings people to make the choices that they do. It is something within them. Even though she felt anger towards what he had done, and there was nothing she could do to make it right, she still had the power to show him a degree of compassion in order to release this from herself. Here is how I taught her to use this tool in that situation.

Example:

I'm sorry I judged you and allowed it to affect me.
Please forgive me for not understanding the kind of pain that must have caused you to make the painful choices that you have.
Thank you
I love you

Remember, there is nothing you can't use this tool on to support healing that needs to take place within yourself. You can even use it to apologize and forgive yourself!

End the healing process by saying this:

"I improve every condition in my life by blessing it"

Apply Encouraging blend or Uplifting blend to your feet after this exercise.

The next two tools are extensive in the healing process. We highly recommend you have someone reading them to you to guide you through them so that you are able to relax and take in the full affects of the healing process, therefore they are written in script form.

Healing Tool #4

Letting Go of Your Prisoners by Janet Conner ("Release Your Prisoners" guided meditation used with permission of the author, Janet Conner, author of *Writing Down Your Soul, The Lotus and The Lily, Soul Vows*, and *The Soul Discovery Coloring Book)*

Suggested Oils you will need for this healing tool:

Renewing Blend - this oil contains of blend of oils that promote forgiveness and a letting go of old wounds from the past that have festered the soul. It is freeing and creates a sense of feeling grounded
Comforting Blend- this oil helps in consoling the soul and to help it heal from loss and the effects of grief, helps in releasing trauma from the past
Thyme - helpful in dissolving pain and anger and softening the bitter heart in order to forgive

Calming Blend - this oil contains a blend that is helpful in forgiving the self and others and releasing grudges of the past and letting go of control

Comforting Blend - this oil helps in consoling the soul and to help it heal from loss and the effects of grief, helps in releasing trauma from the past

Geranium- helps in creating trust in ourselves and in others and the ability to love again and allowing the heart to heal

Peppermint- helps to uplift the heavy heart and bring energy to the soul. It lightens those who feel weary and creates joy and a positive outlook

Oregano- (use with caution-this is a hot oil)- assists in releasing deep seeded anger and towards self and others, helps in letting go of pride and control

Bergamot- Restores confidence in self and acceptance of body and encourages confidence

For after the exercise:

Reassuring Blend- promotes peace and the courage to release fear and find courage within the self

Encouraging blend- this oil motivates the soul to want to create and to bring clarity of purpose to mind body and soul and the energy to carry it out

Uplifting blend- this oil lightens the load of heaviness in the soul and creates an uplifting mood and the ability to let go of the things that weigh us down.

To purchase essential oils please go to
www.aromaheal.org

Place a drop of your oil of choice on your feet, your heart and your gut before using this tool. Diffuse any oil of your choosing to accelerate the healing taking place emotionally through the limbic system as you inhale the oils that are diffused. This can also be used instead of applying the oil topically in case you have an aversion to any oils.

This was a transformational tool for me that I have used on myself and others. It increases the awareness of areas where we still hold onto resentment, anger and pain. We literally keep ourselves prisoner by not releasing it. This is a tool that requires quieting the mind and envisioning what you are looking to release and heal within yourself. It is a powerful tool in self-forgiveness as well. I love how healing this tool really is and how you can use it as often as you need to in order to forgive and release.

You can listen to the recording of this powerful tool at: http://janetconner.com/janet-reads-from-the-lotus-and-the-lily/

Exercise

Find a comfortable and quiet place to do this exercise and either sit or lay down for the duration of it.

You will want to read through this first before beginning if someone is not reading and guiding you through it.

Set your intention for this tool.

A good intention would be "My intention is to let go and forgive all those who have hurt me and to also seek forgiveness within myself."

Stand up to stretch out your dungeon- your lower gut. Put your hands in front of your dungeon, as if they were two heavy doors. Close your eyes.

Then slowly open your hands. As they open, see the long cold dim stairway leading down to your dungeon. Slowly walk down the stone steps. The air gets colder and colder as you descend. There is barely enough light to see. Be careful. Don't slip. Touch the wall to help you.

At the bottom of the stairs is a huge, old, heavily scarred wooden door. The entrance to your dungeon. Haul it open. You are the only one who can.

As the door creaks open, stale putrid air assaults you. The smell is unbearable. The air is even colder and damper than that of the stairway. There is very little light. As your eyes adjust, step over the threshold.

You are now in your dungeon. Look around. Notice the black prison cells lining the walls of your dungeon. (Pause) You may be surprised at how many there are.

Walk up to the first cell. Look at your prisoner. You see who it is. You know why you locked up this prisoner and when. The prisoner has been in your dungeon a long time. (Pause) Now it's time to let your prisoner go. (Pause)

Reach out and open the cell door. You are the only one who can. Look your prisoner in the eye for a moment, then motion for your prisoner to leave. Wave your arm; point to the door. No talking. You don't have to explain. You don't have to go over the old story. You don't even have to apologize. Just let your prisoner go. Your prisoner may hesitate. Wave your prisoner away, saying silently, "You are free. You can go now. Go. Go." (Pause)

Walk up to the next cell. Look at your prisoner. You know who it is. Open the door. Motion for your prisoner to leave. "You're free. Go now. Go." (Pause)

Then walk up to the next cell. You know what to do. Recognize your prisoner, open the door, and let your prisoner go. Do that. (Pause.)

Then go to the next cell and the next and the next and the next. Let all your prisoners go.

When all your prisoners have gone, stop and look around at the rows of empty cells. (Pause)

But wait, you're not finished. You have one more prisoner.

Walk to the very back of your dungeon. Look. There in the corner, in the darkest, darkest, coldest, most miserable cell, is your longest suffering prisoner. (Pause) Look at your prisoner. Look, do you see who it is? (Pause)

It's you. It's always been you. You have kept yourself prisoner for years. You've held yourself prisoner for all the things you think you cannot be forgiven for.

Open the cell. Open it! Say to your prisoner self. "Up. Up. Get up now. You're free." And let yourself go. (Pause)

Now at last your dungeon is empty. Look at all the vacant cells. Lean back slightly and call on the loving power of Spirit to flood your dungeon with white and gold light. Watch as the cells dissolve and the space is filled with warm, loving, healing light. When the space is completely transformed from dark to light, from cold to warm, from prison to chapel, say thank you and open your eyes.

After you have completed this tool sit down and rest. Take a moment to register how you feel about this experience, then write about it.

This release is available every time you return to empty your dungeon.

After you have completed this healing tool apply Reassuring Blend, Encouraging Blend or Uplifting blend to your feet.

Healing Tool #5

Healing Inner Divinity

Our inner divinity is the white light we were born with. It's the God given life force of goodness within us. It is our virtue and power to create. It is our wholeness and the essence of our truth and who we are to our very core. It is the creative life force that connects us to God and love in its purest form. It is self love and dignity and respect and the power to be our truest selves at all times. It is the power of abundance and the flow of life in an easy, vibrant, natural way that has no resistance. It is pure light and grace and in the place we have our strongest inner knowing. If we are not careful, it is what we give away sometimes when we enter into relationships that are not for our highest good.

We all have a beautiful distinct color within us that is our very own. It makes us unique and allows us to stand out. We shine with our own individuality and distinctness. As we enter into certain relationships, our color, or energy, intermingles with others and we lose some of our own defining color. If we aren't careful, we start to mix our energy and give a part of ourselves here and a part of ourselves there and even forget who we've given it to. Sometimes, we even take some energy from others and it gets intermingled with our own. On and on we go until we get to a point that we start to wonder what color we ever were in the first place and who we truly are anymore.

The best comparison I can think of is watercolor painting as a child. I remember having my own brand new watercolor paint set at school. It had all bright pretty individual colors and each color had its own hue of the rainbow. The first time I started painting with it, I took my brush in hand and dipped it into one color. But then I wanted to use a different color, so without rinsing the brush, I dipped it into the second color and the first color began to mix with it. Even when I tried rinsing the brush in water, the colors mingled and never went back to the vibrant colors they started as. The more I painted, the more the colors mixed together and eventually, they lost their original color completely, and the pretty colors weren't so pretty anymore. They became this blackish brownish color and there was no longer any distinction of color. Just like those water colors, this is the same characteristic our energy begins to take if we are not careful.

Let's look even further into what can happen in our intimate relationships with others.

Though our bodies are physical, we are energetic beings as well. When you are intimate with anyone, you merge with their energy. The most powerful way in which energy is exchanged is when we have an intimate or sexual relationship with someone. That is the highest form in which energy is exchanged, through sexual intercourse. Be especially mindful of who you share your intimate energy with sexually. Intimacy at this level intertwines your energy with that of the other person and your energies merge and are absorbed in each other. As it is absorbed, it can bind you energetically together. In a marriage, this is a beautiful thing as it allows husband and wife to become one. In a casual relationship, however, it can be harmful and even damaging when the physical relationship is over because you are still connected energetically.

Regardless of how insignificant you think they are, sexual encounters leave a debris of spiritual energy with you. The more you interact intimately with someone, the deeper the connection and the more their energy becomes intertwined with yours. No matter which way you choose to be intimate, you absorb some of their energy and they absorb some of yours. You carry with you energetically, the energy debris of every person you have become intimate with and they take from you a portion of your energy to carry. Imagine the mixed energy of those who sleep with multiple partners and carry around these multiple energies.

What you may not realize is that those you encounter can have the energy of others intermingled with theirs, because of the people they have been intimate with in their life. Some can feel that energy which can repel positive energy and attract negative energy into your life. Keep in mind that if they have been with multiple partners, you are also absorbing the energy of those multiple partners as they have taken in their energy in the energy exchange between them. These connections, debris and imprints are left upon the soul, mind and spirit for a long time because they are not easily cleansed or purged. When a man or a woman decides to have sex with multiple partners, it can send mixed emotional signals within the body's vibration system.

Even those who have participated in pornographic media are affected. Recall how we pointed out previously that emotional stimuli attaches to an experience and is stored in long term memory. The effect of the memory stays stored within us and, again, energy can get stuck that needs to be released. When you have stimuli that has a greater emotional response pertaining to sexual arousal, like pornographic material, the memory contains even more powerful non beneficial energy because you have stimulated your senses. Participating in any sexual act, be it even over the phone, opens your spirit and energy to receive that sexual energy from another person. Participating in sexual arousal through any of your senses opens the channel of energy between you and the person who aroused you.

Whether you realize it or not, pornographic material affects your energy in a profoundly negative way. As you partake of a sexual act through emotion and fantasy, and entertain sexual thoughts of someone else, you call that person's energy into your presence. Your energy intermingles with theirs through the sexual thought of them and stimulates your senses creating that channel to once again open up. Since your subconscious does not discern fact from fiction, it keeps the imprint of the memory of sex through reality or fantasy and records it as fact. Therefore, the memory of that sexual act between you and the subject of the pornography, is recalled as if it actually happened, and in that, your energy is affected. Sexual desire is the most powerful human emotion. You activate this through pornography.

Time and space do not matter in the energetic realm, as we are all connected to each other. That is how I am able to do phone sessions long distance all over the world because I can tap into someone's energy and spirit in the spiritual realm where you do not have to be physically present for me to see your energetic blocks. The same principles are in effect when you view pornography. Your spirit is intermingling with theirs energetically and you are both affected by it. Effects of pornography can be intermingled with your spirit. Even when you just have sex with someone who has dabbled in it.

We are all connected on an energetic level because we were all formed from the same Creator. It's like your family, even if you aren't close emotionally, you are still related to each other genetically. Our spirits are all related to the same Creator that created us all and placed us here upon the earth. We are connected energetically. When you use pornographic material you are intermingling energetically as you are energetically connected in some way. Sexual relations, in any way, intermingles your spirit with another and binds you together through spiritual energy.

"I always say, never sleep with someone you wouldn't want to be."
-Lisa Chase Patterson

Even experiences of sexual trauma can intermix with, and damage our energy. When we have been violated sexually, our energy has been intermingled with someone else's and the effects can be detrimental emotionally. In cases where we did not give our consent to sexual acts, we may experience trauma not only from the violation, but also the trauma of our energy literally being pulled from us without permission. All sexual encounters, whether consented to or not, leave energetic handprints on our spirit.

Imagine someone has black paint on their hands and they touch you with it. The longer it stays on you, the harder it is to remove it because it dries up. If you have handprints from several people, it can be even more work to remove the paint from your body. This is the same with others energy you have intermingled with sexually. It stays there until you cleanse and clear it off. This is what this beautiful exquisite exercise does- cleanses the divine nature of the self.

This tool was revealed to me in small phases that one day fit together perfectly like pieces to a puzzle and when it came I was overwhelmed with gratitude when I realized the ripple effect it will have on the world. Such deep cleansing and healing is programmed into this tool to heal your spirit and soul you almost feel like you are in a different body. Deep releasing programs are integrated into it for your highest good. It was given and revealed to me as a gift to gift the world. As I have used it on my clients it has been a transformational tool for them. I had one woman who had a husband deeply embedded in and addicted to pornography and it was transformational in healing her but also in helping him to purge the darkness it had brought to his soul.

This tool helps you let go of the energy of others that does not belong to you. It helps you keep integrity with your present relationship by eliminating all negative ties you have to past relationships and clears you of the energies from the past that may have intermingled with yours. It opens the space to create a deeper and authentic relationship with your current relationship. It also supports to release the debris of the trauma that may have been caused when someone violated your own energy. It frees you to feel complete in yourself and in your own wholeness and present in your own spiritual energy and brings pivotal healing to yourself and others. It creates a distinction of your own beautiful vibrancy and empowers you to feel the wholeness of your soul and energy.

It cleanses and washes away the imprints that were not meant to be with yours and creates clarity and purity from experiences you were violated in. Lastly, it makes pristine, your own beautiful precious and sacred inner divinity. Our inner divinity is ours to reclaim and use. This tool helped a client I was working with heal some deep seeded beliefs that she had about her body and her femininity. I cannot say enough about this amazing tool.

The suggested oils you will need for this tool are:

Inspiring Blend- the oil for finding your passion, to heal intimately and let go of sexual setbacks

Comforting Blend- this oil helps in consoling the soul and to help it heal from loss and the effects of grief, helps in releasing trauma from the past

Reassuring Blend- promotes peace and the courage to release fear and find courage within the self

Jasmine- the oil of sexual purity and balance, promotes healthy sexuality, unresolved sexual trauma

Rose- this oil opens the heart to create pure unconditional love and allow a deep connection with their Creator

Melissa- assists in clearing away darkness and allows for light to come into the heart and soul

White Fir- helps to release patterns that have been passed on through the family line generationally and breaks toxic cycles

Suggested oils to use after this exercise:

Encouraging blend- this oil motivates the soul to want to create and to bring clarity of purpose to mind body and soul and the energy to carry it out

Uplifting blend- this oil lightens the load of heaviness in the soul and creates an uplifting mood and the ability to let go of the things that weigh us down. It brings cheer to the soul.

To purchase essential oils please please go to

www.aromaheal.org

Exercise

This tool has two distinct phases and is not complete until you have performed both parts. This exercise has many healing properties programmed into the words spoken in order for healing to take place on all layers and all levels, therefore it is important to speak out loud all the words as you are directed to do so. It magnifies the healing taking place within.

Set your intention for this tool before you begin.

Put the essential oils of your choosing on your heart, gut, and feet before this exercise. Diffuse any oil of your choosing to accelerate the healing taking place emotionally through the limbic system as you inhale the oils that are diffused. This can also be used instead of applying the oil topically in case you have an aversion to any oils.

Sit in a quiet space or lie down in a place where you will have no distractions.

Take several cleansing breaths in and out to relax yourself. Feel your whole body relax as you breathe deeply.

Close your eyes and imagine wrapping yourself in a warm cozy blanket of love. Trust that this whole process is for your highest good and that you will find healing in this tool. Trust that you are safe.

Be gentle and kind to yourself, full of love, and forgiveness. (Pause)

Imagine to yourself all the places in which you have let your energy go. (Pause) Times when you let go of your power and gave up your voice and who you are. (Pause) Times when you let go of you. (Pause) Realize you have the power to call it all back to you. Even your inner divinity. (Pause)

Acknowledge any part that you have had in this and ways in which you felt your energy violated or taken from you as well. (Pause)

Love yourself through this experience. There is a way to clear this as well and to heal from within so that it no longer has any power over you. Today you get to embrace yourself, love yourself and take back your power. (Pause) Take a deep breath in.

In order to send any energy back that you have intermingled with, or that has intermingled with you, we are now going to do the first phase of releasing.

Repeat these words out loud:

"I now let go, and am released from everything and everyone that is no longer part of the divine plan of my life. I release any and all energies that have intermingled with mine that are not for my highest good. I bless them and ask that they be filled with pure love and light and send them back to the spirit from which they came, that pure love and light may increase within them a thousand fold. I ask that anything that has been violated within either of us be healed so that we may all feel complete and whole. I ask that any darkness be taken to the light. We are each healed generationally. This space within each of us is now filled with love and light."

Important:

Take a deep breath in, then exhale. Relax and continue these breaths as many times as you feel you need to repeat them. This allows for all the non-beneficial experiences and emotions to release from your body. These cleansing breaths are what releases it all from your energy. Feel the release and let me know when you are ready for the second phase of this healing tool. (Pause for as long as needed, allowing for it all to release. If any tears flow, just allow it.)

Second phase of this tool:

You are now going to call your energy back to you and hold it in a sacred space before you. Take a deep relaxing breath. (Pause) With your eyes closed, imagine a beautiful white ball of exquisite light and healing energy right in front of you, full of unconditional pure love. (Pause) This is the brightest light you have ever seen. It is love in its purest form. It is Divine Love. It is cleansing, healing and freeing. It is a safe place for your spirit to dwell.

We are going to call back your energy from all the energies it has intermingled with that were not for your highest good. Picture it however you want to. (Pause) You may even just feel it. (Pause) As we call it back, watch every aspect of you that you gave away, return again as it fills up within this white ball of light to be cleansed and purified.

Repeat out loud:

"Everything and everyone that is no longer part of the divine plan of my life now releases me, and are free to go their own way. I call back my own inner divinity and virtue and parts of my spirit and energy that I have given away or have been taken from me and any parts of myself that I have intermingled with others that were not for my highest good, and I treasure what they are to me." (Pause)

Take a deep breath in. Imagine all these parts of you gathered in this safe place. In this ball of light. Give yourself a little time to allow all those parts to gather in.

As you acknowledge these parts and picture them in front of you gathered in, say, "I'm sorry, please forgive me, thank you, I love you." (Pause.) This releases any hold you have on not forgiving yourself.

With your eyes still closed, picture all these energies in front of you being pulled into the white ball of light. Imagine all these parts of your energy being washed and cleansed and purified within this ball of light and gathered in this place of safety. Any debris is released from those you intermingled with. Watch as each aspect of your energy that has been separated or intermingled with any other person is encompassed with pure love and divine light. It is pure and bright and clean as it goes through this cleansing process. Say this out loud: "I am worthy to be clean." (Pause) When you feel complete with the cleansing let me know.

(Wait to get confirmation they are complete)

Take the ball of light into your hands and feel the love inside of it. Bask in the peace of it. (Pause) Place it in your sacral chakra (your abdomen) and imagine this light spreading throughout your whole body from your abdomen and up to your heart and arms and head and from your abdomen down through your legs and feet until it has filled you completely and you are engulfed in pure light. (Pause)

Now imagine standing under a beautiful, natural, clean waterfall. It contains healing water. You feel its love as it caresses your skin and every part of you. It touches you from head to toe as the water falls around you and upon you. It is washing away all the debris from these experiences that have brought non-beneficial energy with it. Allow it to wash completely over you and to cleanse away the guilt, the shame, the energy of anything that is not for your highest good and any resistance you have had to accepting pure unconditional love for yourself and feel your heart and soul light up. Allow it to cleanse away anything you are holding onto. (Pause)

As you are standing in this beautiful waterfall and feeling cleansed and refreshed, repeat the following words:

Repeat out loud:

"I dissolve and un-create in my own mind and in the minds of all others, any idea that my power or my virtue can be withheld from me. No person, thing or event can keep my inner divinity from me! I heal the inner divinity and essence within me through Divine Love and strengthen the core of who I am. I ask God to restore those parts of me with divine love, pure light and healing and to reverse any damage that has been done."

"I give thanks that my body is a temple of God. I now praise, bless, and glorify divine health in my body and claim my own sacred divinity, my virtue and my power to create! The Divine Love within me creates generational healing within us all. I embrace my own exquisite _____ (femininity) (masculinity)"

"I consecrate my body, my inner divinity, and power to create to the Light that it may increase within me and without me a thousand fold. I am whole." (Pause)

Take a deep breath in and out. Then, another deep breath in and exhale. This breath is very important as it integrates all the healing that you just stated.

Say out loud: "I Choose Peace." "I Choose Love." "I Choose Light." "I am Complete."

Deep breath in.

You are now complete.

Apply Encouraging blend and Uplifting blend to your heart or in the diffuser after this exercise.

Make sure to drink a good amount of water after this tool to move the energy completely out of your body and to get the rest your body needs to release this all. Feel the lightness and the peace.

Conclusion

We hope you have found more enlightenment through the information we have provided you and that it has brought you closer to the truth of who you are on your own healing journey. You deserve to heal and feel whole. When you release and let go, it allows for a space to create light within. May you use this information to increase your own vibration and bring more fulfillment to your life. Pain can keep you prisoner only until you decide to release it and no longer allow it to have power in your life.

Healing is the most powerful gift you can give yourself. We hope you have found fulfillment in the tools we have provided and that you have taken the transformational step of bringing healing to your soul. As you heal through the high vibration of essential oils and on a spirit level, you can truly feel the freedom of healing for yourself at a deeper and more permanent level.

We both have our own private practices as energy healing practitioners. We don't claim to heal you but we do support you with powerful tools to use in your own healing. We know that in order for true healing to take place, you are the one empowering yourself in your own healing. We support and facilitate you in a safe environment for healing through guidance and direction.

We know that in all of these processes and tools, our Creator is the true healer. It is through Him, that healing takes place. If you feel you need healing at a deeper level, please feel free to contact us for a session to do so. We feel strongly that there is a movement and journey we have embarked on to heal the world one drop at a time.

We hope you find the healing we have seen many others already experience. You can read about some of their experiences in the back of the book. The joy we find in watching others experience healing is immeasurable for we know that it has brought them a step closer to seeing their true value and worth and the ability to live their purpose at a higher and more meaningful and fulfilling level than ever before.

We are excited as we bring our Aroma Heal certification to the forefront to spread light and healing all over the world! If you would like to become Aroma Heal certified or even just attend a class where we walk you through the healing tools contained in our books, go to our website www.aromaheal.org to sign up for our newsletter and to receive a schedule of upcoming events, which include our classes and certifications, and free webinars.   Who knows? It might be right in your neighborhood!

Here is to your light, your heart and your healing! Keep shining! The world needs you!

Essential Oils & Emotions

Suggested Essential Oils for the Healing Tools in this book:

Basil-

This is an essential oil to help support those who are feeling overwhelmed or fatigued. It is an oil that allows one to release the temporary perspectives that are weighing them down and to take a step back and view the experiences in their life with a broader view. It allows one to gain a sense of renewal and peace, both physically, mentally, spiritually, and emotionally, as they can better cope with the situations at hand. This renewed strength encourages one to continue on in the work they must do.

Bergamot –

This oil is an uplifting citrus oil that instills a sense of reassurance and confidence regarding the self. It aids individuals in recognizing their personal worth and value and to stand strong in their purpose. It allows them to lovingly view and accept their imperfections and to embrace themselves. It imbues confidence and allows one to let go of a lower belief in self. Through this oil they can see things with a greater confidence in self and purpose.

Cedarwood-

This oil supports those who may feel alone, abandoned, or disconnected from their relationships. It helps them to identify the support system in place around them that may include family, friends, and their community. It supports a sense of belonging and helps to reveal their place and purpose in the relationships around them. This oil provides one to feel more secure, wanted, and supported in all regards, even support from the Divine.

Comforting Blend-

This blend of essential oils is akin to wrapping a blanket of love and support around oneself energetically, emotionally, and spiritually. When feeling down, loss, shame, broken, heartache, abandoned, unloved, or unappreciated, this oil helps to soothe those feelings away in a tender, loving manner. It helps to release those negative emotions and instills a great sense of peace, comfort, love, and light once again in their place. It lifts one to have the strength to continue when challenges come and to increase in faith and recognize their worth.

Encouraging Blend-

This uplifting blend of oils supports those who need an extra boost to motivate them. It helps them to see purpose, power, and vision in what they need to do and the strength, energy, and vigor to take those first steps forward and/or to continue on when they become weary. It helps them to move past whatever it is that is holding them back from taking action; false beliefs, generational patterns, blocks, loss of vision or purpose. This oil brings movement back into their mission, vision, and purpose.

Frankincense –

Frankincense essential oil is a powerful eye-opener and cleanser of spiritual deceptions and darkness. It aids in protecting the soul and aiding in its growth and development. Frankincense aids in creating a positive attachment with one's father, both Divine and mortally. It helps an individual to enhance the greatness of the True Self, healthy masculinity, and draw closer to divinity.

Geranium –

Geranium essential oil has the ability to mend the broken heart and allow one to love and feel love more fully. It encourages reception to trust, love, and reconnection with others when a loss or break in trust in the relationship has occurred. It opens the heart to new possibilities and array of positive emotions.

Inspiring Blend-

This blend of essential oils invites and welcomes passion back into one's life. It instills a sense of purpose in one's heart again. This oil reignites the spark inside in love, life, and purpose. It instills energy and excitement and even a clearer vision for the direction one should move in. It creates a powerful, energetic connection between one and their purpose and can overflow into all aspects; for example, relationships, work, and goals. It contains oils that are sexually healing as well as igniting passion in the intimate aspects of a relationship. This oil ignites the soul-fire, brings joy, excitement, and energy to one and helps them to make the jump they need with vision and vigor.

Jasmine-

Jasmine supports powerful healing for those who have had non-beneficial experiences in regard to their sexuality. This oil especially supports those who may feel shame, broken, damaged, or disgusted with their own sexuality. It uplifts those who have had negative experiences affecting their value and worth connected to their divine power to create and connect with others at a very trusting, loving, open, and intimate level. It helps one to shed these negative emotions and false beliefs tied to previous experiences or generational patterns, and instills a greater sense of peace, connection, and love while sharing in these experiences and strengthening their relationship with the Divine.

Lemongrass-

Lemongrass is an oil that aids in the release of non-beneficial energy. For example, this can come in the form of non-beneficial relationships, false beliefs, generational patterns, or even over-accumulation of material possessions. This release in non-beneficial patterns and energy encourages and opens up a place to welcome in clean, fresh starts and new beneficial beliefs.

Melissa-

This oil that calls in light and beneficial energy and support from the Divine. It sheds darkness, and non-beneficial energy as they cannot dwell in the same place. It helps one to draw closer to the Divine and to see things with a greater light and understanding. It is like a light shining into darkness allowing one to see fully what truly is around them and instead provides peace, comfort, and even direction. It lifts one above their current situation and allows one to gain a greater understanding of their value, purpose, and mission in life more clearly as this oil invites light into their heart and soul.

Oregano -

Oregano essential oil is very powerful both physically and emotionally. It helps to soften the stubborn and strong willed so they are able to more clearly envision their higher purpose and connect to it. It helps to knock down those personal roadblocks so that one can move forward with more ease in collaboration with others. This is oil is beneficial in letting go of low vibration emotions and non beneficial energy. It can help to release deep seeded anger issues. Please note that Oregano is a 'hot' oil and such should always be diluted when being used. Use it with caution.

Peppermint-

Peppermint is an oil that helps to lift one up during difficult times. It allows one to take a reprieve, breather, or break from the stresses or current situations and regain their strength, vigor, and passion before diving back in. This oil is wonderful to help the heart regain the courage it needs to process and fight for the things that are right. It is not recommended to use this oil for continual, on-going use to 'avoid' the issues at hand. One cannot avoid the difficult experiences in life, but with peppermint oil, they can regain the strength, composure, and passion to continue forward.

Reassuring Blend-

This essential oil blend soothes the heart and soul. It envelops one in peace and protection spiritually and emotionally. It creates a safe place where one can move forward with fortitude through the hardships, trials, and experiences life brings. Within the boundaries of this safe-place, one is able to see the blows, attacks, and darts being thrown their way in advance and allows them to prepare for and respond in light and foresight. This oil provides a reassurance in these moments and allows one to see the light and peace that is available at all times.

Renewing Blend-

This essential oil blend uplifts the heart as it softens and washes away the blocks and hardness around it. This oil helps to release the non-beneficial emotions one is holding onto that limit their ability to love completely and also receive love more fully. It cleanses the build-up from past negative experiences that have not been released. It allows one to view their negative experiences within themselves and others from a broader perspective so they can see the role these experiences have played in helping them become who they are now, and to lovingly release them so that they can move forward. As they do so it opens up a space to receive love, acceptance, peace, comfort, and light into their lives more fully.

Rose –

Rose oil is the highest frequency essential oil on earth. This oil invites a person to experience the powerful essence of unconditional love. As an individual opens up their heart to experience greater love and charity, they are able to feel this for oneself and others. Rose oil embodies Divine or unconditional love on all levels and creates a sense of peace and a great softening of the heart.

Thyme –

Thyme essential oil is powerful in cleansing the soul of unresolved anger and bitter feelings. It clears and releases the body and soul of negative emotions that have been buried deep within and opens up to allow the individual to fill themselves with love and light and forgiveness of self and others.

Uplifting Blend-

This blend of essential oils is like the sunlight breaking through the clouds. It instills cheer, happiness, and joy into even the gloomiest of days or moments. It uplifts one to a place where they can release the non-beneficial energy they are holding onto or that may be bringing them down. It reignites one to be able to taste the flavors of all the positive aspects that life has to provide. When one has been dulled from non-beneficial energy or repeated exposure to hardships, this oil helps to provide a sensitivity to the positive and happy experiences one has to offer. They are able to see the light and express more gratitude. This oil blend instills happiness and joy to the soul.

White Fir –

White Fir essential oil allows the self to realize and release negative false beliefs that have been passed on from one generation to another and releasing the cycles from continuing to repeat themselves. It supports a person as they let go of toxicity and brings healing to the mind, body and spirit.

Wintergreen-

This is an oil that helps to ease the pain one is dealing

with. Often our emotional or spiritual blocks or problems begin to manifest themselves physically. This oil helps to identify the true root of the pain and provides a safe place of release for the emotional healing to occur. This can affect a person in all aspects. As they release the non-beneficial, or even painful emotional patterns, their physical body will also feel a release and improvement.

References

1. Skarin, A.(1966) (n.d.). *Man Triumphant* (p. 66). Devorss & Co.

2. Greer, C. (2007, April 14). *Scents and Sensibility: The Molecular Mechanisms of Olfaction.* Lecture presented at Science on Saturday in Yale University. Retrieved 2015, from https://www.youtube.com/watch?v=bsU-H4H_ACo

3. Lanteaume, L., Khalfa, S., Regis, J., Marquis, P., Chauvel, P., & Bartolomei, F. (2006). Emotion Induction After Direct Intracerebral Stimulations of Human Amygdala. *Oxford Journals, 17*(6), 1307-1313. Retrieved 2015, from http://cercor.oxfordjournals.org/content/17/6/1307

4. Amygdala. (2015). Retrieved 2015, from https://en.wikipedia.org/wiki/Amygdala

5. Mercola. (2014, September 4). Essential Oils Support Physical and Emotional Well-Being. Retrieved 2015, from http://articles.mercola.com/sites/articles/archive/2014/09/04/essential-oils-aromatherapy.aspx

6. Hill, D. (2015, October 26). The Science of Emotional Aromatherapy. Retrieved 2015, from http://doterrascienceblog.com/the-science-of-emotional-aromatherapy/

7. Shakeshaft, J. (2014, July 2). 6 Breathing Exercises to Relax in 10 Minutes or Less. Retrieved from http://greatist.com/happiness/breathing-exercises-relax

8. How To Use Your Emotions To Heal. (n.d.). Retrieved 2015, from http://www.silvamindbodyhealing.com/online/lessons/healing-techniques

9. Forgiveness: Letting go of grudges and bitterness. (2014, November 11). Retrieved 2015, from http://www.mayoclinic.org/healthy-living/adult-health/in-depth/forgiveness/art-20047692

10. Emoto, M. (2005, September 1). The Hidden Messages in Water. Retrieved 2015, from http://www.superconsciousness.com/topics/environment/hidden-messages-water#sthash.mAyqErau.dpuf

11. Greenleaf, C. (2011). *Re-Entering Eden: Reclaiming Our Wholeness and Divine Truth*. Balboa Press.

12. Ho'oponopono. (2015). Retrieved 2015, from https://en.wikipedia.org/wiki/Hoʻoponopono

The Healing Coach

www.thehealingcoach.com

Christi Turley Diamond B.S., M.Ed. has a background in psychology and working with people who have had deep traumatic loss in their lives and many others who are just looking to gain a new outlook on life and let go of the past. She has worked with many clients that have experienced loss in a variety of ways. Christi says "We are taught how to acquire things and relationships but not how to deal with the loss of them. The way we deal with loss is usually taught to us by how our parents or caregivers dealt with loss and many times this misinformation and legacy of mistakes is passed on from generation to generation. As a result, we never really grieve the losses in our lives or feel complete. This can leave a hole in our hearts that seems to gape open at times; we are often overcome with heart-wrenching grief that leaves us feeling hollow inside."

Christi trained with life coaches and energy healers and learned a variety of modalities and then through her own work began realizing that clients were doing a lot of the right things but what held them back from progressing forward were the false beliefs they were carrying with them. They might have great goals to make a fortune but somewhere in their belief system was the belief that they weren't worthy of money so somehow they would sabotage receiving money. Another client would have patterns of getting into bad relationships and couldn't recognize why they kept having the same kinds of relationships over and over and they felt stuck. It all went back to their belief system and Christi recognized that clearing these old beliefs was a key factor to them finally becoming successful financially or in relationships or whatever area they were being held back in. She became very intuitive to finding where the problem might lie and helping clients to clear and release so they could heal and move forward.

Through study and experience she also realized that emotions can get stuck in the body in a place where they have never completely processed and they lie stagnant keeping people from progressing and maturing in aspects of their relationship in areas they don't feel complete or ways in which they push love away.

She says, "What stems from not fully allowing ourselves to grieve or process our emotions is an incompleteness within ourselves, a pain that can eat away at us for years. Because of this pain, we rob ourselves of living in the moment and become prisoners to the hold the past has on us. We end up with anxiety over our future and the fear of losing something else, denying ourselves the opportunity to feel joy and peace and live in the here and now."

Through energy healing and using essential oils, Christi has seen lives change completely and people heal who have held onto things for years. She knows the work she does can literally be transformational and life changing. She has clients all over the country that she does phone sessions with in an hour's time, and she sees results they haven't seen sometimes in years of therapy.

Christi Turley Diamond is dedicated to helping people heal. As they do, they are able to let go, find their purpose and live their passions. She finds her life work very fulfilling and feels privileged in doing it. She knows that God does all the healing and she has the honor of being the instrument to facilitate that. She helps people release blocks that hold them back. She helps to clear and release emotional blocks regarding relationships, money, health and many others. She is the bridge from where you are to where you want to be and she coaches you in clearing barriers and then getting to your desired destination. Here are a few testimonials from those who have experienced her healing sessions:

"Few people allow their senses to guide their lives and even fewer take their gifts and share it with others. Christi Turley Diamond is one such person. Christi is a supportive teacher and a trust-worthy confidant. Her spiritual insight and training have allowed me to make progress in my life. I have made great strides in forgiving, processing loss and developing hope. I sailed through life more by chance than plan, never sure why I reacted the way I did to situations. I avoided looking too close at my past because the loss and pain were simply too great. In my simplistic way of handling things, I blamed myself for my poor choices and lived my life consumed with regret and avoidance. Through some emotional excavations, I realized I had carried learned traits from my childhood into my relationships. Christi has helped me to recover my memories, analyze the past, process the pain and learn to forgive and bring healing to past experiences I thought could never feel healed from. She introduced me to some powerful tools I could use in order to heal any relationship I still needed closure in. I no longer need to live in a state of avoidance and regret. I can now have hope and peace. Life is a journey; Christi is helping me navigate successfully through the roadblocks and enjoy the trip."

- TerryKay D.

"Some things that have been weighing on my heart and soul for my lifetime were literally lifted within just a couple of hours. This is something I have been working to do for years but had been unsuccessful until working with Christi. I am so excited to move forward without carrying that additional weight around on my mind and in my heart. Christi you are truly gifted!"
- H.M.

"I had a session with Christi Turley Diamond and it was truly life changing. I honestly didn't know what to expect from a session with her. I went in thinking there may not be much to uncover but soon realized I had pushed things from my past down deeply and I needed healing in to move forward in all aspects of my life, especially my business. She instructed me to apply certain oils and I went to bed still processing. The next morning I woke up feeling light and bright. I have had my productivity in my business improve a TON and the relationships with my family, husband and children change dramatically and I feel more open to love and support. I know it is all a process and takes time to heal. I am truly looking forward to scheduling another session as soon as possible"
- C.W.

"I have come to know Christi as an Angel among us. I found her on such a coincidental journey, or better yet God sent her to us. I say us because I feel like she is helping to save our entire family. I am embarrassed to say I had little knowledge into energy healing and work with the other side and quite honestly I would have likely not believed the value of it. However, within our first conversation Christi changed my entire view on this world we live in. She knew so many thing and truths that I have not shared with a soul. She brought me up from a crater I didn't even realize I had fallen into. Throughout our journey Christi has helped me with my four year old son who has been to play therapists, psychologists, psychiatrists and occupational therapists. She has literally done more for him in our few sessions than all those professionals could do within the past year. She has also strengthened my marriage and helped me find myself, my joy, my value and my strengths. I can honestly say Christi likely saved me and my entire family. If you are the least unsure about her gift the best thing you could do for yourself and your loved ones is try. She truly is an Angel among us with a very precious gift."

- Amber Brown

"Christi Turley Diamond is a true gift to this world where so many are hurting. Her ability to inspire clients and audiences to become more, to overcome obstacles and to truly connect to their highest self, is nothing short of miraculous. I

recommend her to anyone who is seeking the light in their lives, who feel broken, down and out, and those who are not living up to their immeasurable privileges. To coach with her is to take a quantum leap in the right direction!"
-Lisa Walker, (creator of *Transform Your Results* International Speaker and Author)

"Christi has empowered and assisted me during some of my most difficult times. She has real life experience, education and a gift for helping people regain clarity and most importantly HOPE in times of crisis. She has successfully walked me through my grief during times of darkness that I felt were impossible to get through. Christi has been a powerful guide in my journey to reconnecting to my authentic self, recognizing what my dreams and goals are and taking practical steps towards living a life I love."
-Ang B.

"Christi was able to clear something that had been plaguing my marriage for 21 years and she was able to do it one hour's time. That is how powerful energy healing can be! It changed my life!"
-Heather Madder (Author, International Speaker, Business Coach)

Christi Turley Diamond B.S., M.Ed. is a Grief Recovery Specialist, an Energy Healer and Life

Coach. She facilitates sessions over the phone with clients nationwide individually and in group sessions. If you have experienced loss or need to delve further into deeper healing you can schedule a session with her at www.thehealingcoach.com.

www.KarisaTomkinson.com

Karisa Tomkinson, B.S., M.S. has always loved working with and serving others and uplifting them to a higher state. It really sparked while working as a therapist and seeing the life changing impact that others experienced physically. The quality of life was literally transformed as she worked in this arena.

When Karisa began working with essential oils, little did she know the same service and transformational work would continue with every person she worked with. Whether as a business partner or as a customer, she has grown to see the power one person can make. It is truly a ripple effect that spreads quickly when one person realizes their value, worth, and potential. God has a divine role, a mission, a great purpose and NEED for every single person.

Karisa says "It is almost as if you are standing in front of a door with a beautiful view on the other side of the window. You can look through the window and are able to admire all you see. You are grateful for the view and may or may not even realize that the beauty extends beyond the view the window shows." Karisa helps you to know that there is more within that window of yourself and your potential. You may not have a key or know how to even unlock it though. Karisa helps to unlock the door you stand before. It is a door that opens to discovering the greater aspects of the self. It is a door to releasing limiting beliefs and growing closer to God. You then are able to walk through and see a greater perspective and view of what is before you. She is a person who empowers others with their own reality of worth, gifts, and potential through coaching, using essential oils, and special healing gifts she attributes to God.

Here are a few testimonials from those she has worked with in various arenas and areas of their lives:

"Karisa Tomkinson is an inspiration. She has inspired me to become my best self. She has educated me on essential oils and the powerful effects they have, both physically and emotionally, and I love using them for both. Her support and motivation to help me live a healthier life has helped me to do just that. On the other side of things, she has a great spirit and is very in tune with the Lord. She has given me inspired advice countless times and has helped me sort through my own thoughts and feelings; to better understand myself and my emotions. [These things] work. They are therapeutic and bring peace and healing. I am so grateful to have them as a healing tool in my life."
– Kristianna Crawford

"I started to have an anxiety attack, and also was experiencing withdrawals from my depression medication while sight seeing with Karisa and our families. Karisa had me sit down on a nearby bench and while giving me some essential oils to use, told me to tap my head in different spots while saying specific affirmations and then tap my chest, again with affirmations of a kind. She had me do this 3-4 times. I recall the first time I didn't feel much different, but was grateful for the help. However, by the 3rd and 4th times, I was calm, collected, and feeling back in control of myself. I was so grateful for her guidance to help me help myself. She acted perfectly in the situation to fit my needs. Love her and the tools of healing and essential oils!"
– Krystal Amundsen

"Karisa is an amazing leader and a very inspiring woman! She has mentored me in my business and has also helped me in better understanding my own personal gifts and talents and how to use them to help other people. I have had several clearing sessions with her and I feel she has such a strong intuition and my time with her was very insightful! She helped me to clear my fear of success and fear of failure, both of which were big blocks that were holding me back from progressing in my business and as an individual. With these blocks out of the way, I now feel empowered to create whatever I want from life! I

have since seen unprecedented growth in my business and have even been promoted three times in two months. Karisa has an amazing ability to see the potential in an individual and to inspire them to get out of their comfort zone and go for it!"
-Megan Watson

"I have used essential oils for over three years, but mostly for the physical health benefits. Karisa Tomkinson has helped me as a mentor and coach while teaching me more about the use of essential oils for the emotional benefits. I never really understood the scope of how essential oils can be used for their healing components with my emotions, but there are several oils I use on a regular basis for all different types of emotions I have experienced. Karisa is such a compassionate person in my life and a light in this sometimes crazy world. I'm thankful for her caring heart!!"
-Lori Swift

If you would like to connect with Karisa for more insight on discovering and uncovering your own amazing potential stored within to greater capacities, she can be reached at www.KarisaTomkinson.com.

About The Authors

Christi Turley Diamond B.S., M.Ed., is a Speaker, Author, Energy Healer, Life Coach and Grief Coach. She worked for years in a non-profit organization assisting many affected by loss and trauma and provided services to support them in their healing. She obtained several awards for her work with the organization. She is certified as a Grief and Loss Recovery Specialist. She does individual phone sessions and group sessions with clients all over the world and is traveling the country with her husband and daughter as they connect with other healers and share their vision of healing with the world. She and Karisa are excited to be bringing Aroma Heal certification to the world! This is part of her passion as she travels the country to help many become Aroma Heal certified, strengthen their own light and then spread that light and healing to others. She has been trained in a variety of modalities and says that she pulls from her "energetic toolbox" in each session she does. She has worked with hundreds to help them on their own journey to heal. She has her Bachelor's degree in Psychology and her Master's degree in Instructional Design/Education. She has been teaching in a variety of ways for many years and enjoys educating others about the healing properties of pure essential oils. It is her passion to help others let go of pain in order to serve their purpose. Her purpose is to increase light upon the earth as she helps others recognize theirs. You can find her on her website at www.thehealingcoach.com. When she is not doing sessions, she is spending time with her four amazing children and her supportive husband. Traveling and road trips are part of her fun and adventurous side. She is truly fascinated by people, their story and their courage in overcoming, for she finds them inspiring! Time with her family is what she treasures most.

Karisa Tomkinson B.S., M.S., is an Occupational Therapist and a wellness advocate currently residing in Arizona. Health is an important aspect of her lifestyle. Her work in Occupational Therapy has enlightened her with valuable knowledge about the body and what is necessary for it to function at its optimum level by what you put into it and how you physically take care of it. She loves working one on one with patients and empowering them in their lives through the therapy she provides. She began using essential oils as they complimented her studies and knowledge as a therapist and has grown in her passion for the healing and emotional aspect they provide. She teaches webinars worldwide about the emotional healing properties of essential oils and is well versed in this area. She has designed and managed her own retail store and is a photographer, but mostly loves her work mentoring and coaching an international business team. She is also expanding her own healing business as she is soon to be training many to be Aroma Heal certified and doing sessions of her own with clients across the country. You can learn more about her on her website www.KarisaTomkinson.com. She has two kids and in her free time she enjoys traveling, road biking, long distance running, and being outdoors. She is outgoing, devoted to her faith and family, and lives her life on purpose!